advance praise for
the knack OF A HAPPY LIFE

"Luleen Anderson's *Knack* inspires without becoming preachy or sentimental. She tells good stories about real people that together form a comprehensive curriculum in happiness. Good for armchairs, hammocks, porches, bathrooms, beach blankets, and planes." —Peggy Payne, author of *Sister India* and coauthor of *The Healing Power of Doing Good*

"What a rare combination! Luleen Anderson's book is as serious of purpose as it is entertaining to read, with nuggets of wisdom on every page."

—Ellyn Bache, author of *Holiday Miracles* and *Safe Passage*

"When you come across a sharecropper's daughter, reared dirt-poor, who got a Ph.D., became a therapist, a published writer—you want to know the secrets of her success. Some of the wisest words are also the most simple, and here are her simple, wise, accessible secrets to the knack of a happy life. Her words will resonate in you long after you put down the book." —Sophy Burnham, author of *A Book of Angels*

"There is great beauty and wisdom in this work." —author Daniel Ladinsky, translator of *The Gift: Poems by Hafiz* and others

"Clinical psychologist Luleen Anderson has the gift of writing clearly about complex human relationships. She does not bypass suffering but shows us the way to happiness, in the spirit of the Dalai Lama's *The Art of Happiness*. She makes available both to professionals and to the ordinary reader her lifetime of academic and clinical expertise."

—Jenny Yates, Ph.D., author of *Jung on Death and Immortality*

"Gentle humor and clarity of insight make *The Knack* not only an enjoyable book but a very wise one as well." —Catherine McCall, M.D., psychiatrist and author of *Lifeguarding: A Memoir of Secrets, Swimming, and the South*

nine lessons along the journey

LULEEN S. ANDERSON

Published by Winoca Press
P. O. Box 30, Wilmington, NC 28402-0300 USA
www.winocapress.com

Available direct from the publisher, from your local bookstore, or from the author at www.luleenanderson.com

Printed in the United States of America
09 08 07 5 4 3 2 1 a

Library of Congress Cataloging-in-Publication Data

ISBN 978-0-9789736-3-6

Book cover and interior designed by Barbara Brannon; cover image used by permission of Barbara Brannon

Epigraphs from the poems of Hafiz are taken from "Your Seed Pouch," "To Build a Swing," "Today," "A Great Need," "The Stairway of Existence," "Find a Better Job," "That Shapes the Eye," and "Your Mother and My Mother" in *The Gift: Poems by Hafiz, The Great Sufi Master,* translated by Daniel Ladinsky (Penguin Compass, 1999); "Strange Miracle" and "I Am Determined" in *I Heard God Laughing: Renderings of Hafiz,* by Daniel Ladinsky (Dharma Printing, 1996); "The Happy Virus" in *The Subject Tonight Is Love: 60 Wild and Sweet Poems of Hafiz,* versions by Daniel Ladinsky (Pumpkin House Press, 1996).

For Glenn

Also by Luleen S. Anderson, Ph.D.

Sunday Came Early This Week

Fill Me Up to Empty

Under the Covers

Contents

When all your desires are distilled
You will cast just two votes:

To love more,
And be happy.

—from *The Gift: Poems by Hafiz, The Great Sufi Master,*
translated by Daniel Ladinsky

Acknowledgments

THIS BOOK HAS BEEN INFLUENCED BY MANY PEOPLE. I am especially grateful to *Wilma!* Magazine publisher Joy Allen and former *Wilma!* editor Marita Bon for inviting me to write a monthly column for the magazine, and for Marita's careful editing of many of the columns. The four-year-plus collaboration with them, as well as the enthusiasm of the magazine's readership, has been heartwarming.

Almost all of the chapters included in this book have appeared in some form in *Wilma!*. Two appeared originally, under different titles, in the *Boston Globe* ("Teddy Bears" and "Take My Hand"). "Why Can't You Just Listen to Me?" appeared in the *Wesleyan Advocate.* Other versions of "Under the Covers," "Why Can't You Just Be a Teacher?," and "Gracelets" appeared originally in my book *Under the Covers.* "Learn from Suffering," "The Good-Enough Parent," and "When Children Face Grief" are new in this collection.

Several people read earlier drafts and offered helpful suggestions, including Jenny Yates, Margit Royal, Susan Roscher, Catherine McCall, and Nan Cameron. My deepest appreciation goes to Glenn Barefoot, whose unwavering support and gentle but insistent prodding improved every *Wilma!* column. Her fierce determination that *The Knack* be shared with others, and her ideas about how to make it happen, helped shape this work. Her influence permeates every page.

I am grateful to Daniel Ladinsky, who years ago introduced me to the Persian poet Hafiz through his renderings in several books. Since then, both he and Hafiz have become cherished friends, and I have chosen some of my favorite Hafiz quotes to open each section.

I owe a special thanks to Barbara Brannon for her enthusiastic support, and to all those who invited me into their lives and allowed me to share in their journey.

Finally, I am indebted to my son, Eric, who contributes much to my own knack of a happy life.

Prologue

Learning the Knack

JUDGE NEMA HAD CHOICES TO MAKE. He was fifty-four years old and had been told he was dying of lung cancer. His first decision was to be open about his impending death. Second, he decided he would die happy.

These decisions meant trouble with members of his family, who were furious, since they felt he had brought this problem on himself by being a heavy smoker most of his life. His wife especially railed at him for all his illness would put her through. Their oldest daughter, a college freshman who was painfully aware that her father's past drinking behavior had kept him distant, said through angry tears: "Thanks to you, I'll lose the only Dad I *never* had!"

Judge Nema embraced his daughter as she spewed her disappointment and anger. He vowed to perform her marriage ceremony, which in due time he did from a wheelchair. At the reception, he made it to the ballroom floor and, with a helper rolling his oxygen tank along beside him, he waltzed his daughter around the floor. Two weeks later, he died happy.

Throughout a long, painful, eighteen-month ordeal, Judge Nema expressed joy, laughed at jokes, took pleasure in the birds visiting his feeders, and welcomed a constant stream of guests who were eager just to be in his electrifying presence. He was an authentic human being, accepting his situation and his family's grief, resentment, and love.

In my practice as a clinical psychologist, I counseled the judge's sister, who had been among those resentful of his lifestyle choices. "When the thing he feared most came to pass," she said to me, "he found joy and happiness, and he brought that happiness to all of us, to the whole town." She paused to wonder. "How did he do that?" It is a profound question. What was it about Judge Nema that allowed him to be happy? Was it some special gift or blessing, unknown to the rest of us? Was he so different from most people?

"When I grow up, I want to be like Grandma," twelve-year-old Charles said. "She has the knack of a happy life." What brilliant insight from the mouth of this child!

Having the knack is not a matter of luck. This attitude of acceptance and wonder comes into the world anew with each little baby, but is nurtured or destroyed by experience and exposure. We are fortunate if at each stage of life we have enjoyed the happiness of babies, the thrill of discovery, the awe of nature.

A happy life is possible. The framers of the Declaration of Independence for the emerging United States spoke to this as the right to "life, liberty, and the pursuit of happiness." Why pursue it if it is not attainable? Happiness is an inalienable right because it's an inborn quality. Expressing the knack is more difficult for one born blind or for a crack baby, but it is not out of reach. The knack of happiness is not a fleeting moment. It persists in spite of incredible pain, suffering, and trauma brought on by forces outside our control. It always takes effort in the face of rejection and loss of loved ones—in the face of our own death—to hold on to this core truth: A happy life is our choice. Misery is optional.

The Knack of a Happy Life addresses this simple but vexing question:

"How do we live a happy life?" The answer lies in our ability to accept life on its own terms, to know ourselves and others, and to seek eternal truths about life and living. It is simple, but it is not easy. The wisdom of the ages teaches us that life is about loving and being satisfied. The good news is that happiness lies deep within us, ready to burst forth if we allow it to find expression. The happiness I'm thinking of is not a giggly, temporary state of being. It is the natural joy that comes in spite of our troubles. Of course, giggles are a side benefit, and great for our health.

In my own life I have become acquainted with many people like Judge Nema, and Grandma, and young Charles, who had that enviable knack for happiness. In my teaching and work as a clinical psychologist I have counseled and inspired hundreds of others to choose a meaningful, authentic life for themselves. In these pages you will meet some of them—though with different names and details—real men, women, and children who have faced a particular challenge and triumphed.

The Knack of a Happy Life reveals what I have learned from my personal journey, my clients' experiences, and my contacts with people of all ages who have chosen happy lives under the most trying circumstances. Nine "lessons" follow stages of life and themes that recur for us all between birth and death, and in them are essays and anecdotes springing from actual experiences. These are the stories of people seeking to be happy with themselves, their family of origin, their friends and community, their work and love life, their health and faith and fortunes. They have chosen to live happy lives.

It is my hope that you will find, as I did in reflecting on their challenges and choices, a measure of their same strength and satisfaction. Happiness is a choice we make every day. What does it look like when an individual has the knack of a happy life? Read on. May these portraits help you on your own journey.

the Knack of a *Happy Life*

lesson one

Knowing the Knack When We See It

O wondrous creatures,
By what strange miracle
Do you so often
Not smile?

—HAFIZ

How do we learn the knack of a happy life? We learn from others; we catch it from those who have awareness of it. The knack is a gift from generations past. We learn by standing on the shoulders of giants. We learn from the wisdom literature of the sages. We learn to harness our powerful minds to focus in healthy directions.

The choices we make become building blocks for future generations. Our shoulders will support others. You might think that fact would be enough to make us watch our step pretty carefully. Yet we all stumble and fall at times—it's to be expected. It's not the falling that's important; what's imperative is that we get up and try again, that we reflect on our experiences and gain knowledge from them.

1

Show Me the Way

"YOU'LL NEED A SUITCASE AND SOME NEW CLOTHES before you leave for college," Mary Bradley said as she handed me the first piece of luggage I had ever owned. "I'll take you to Macon tomorrow and get you some things at Belk's."

Mary Bradley was an artist and the owner of the Bogus Bank. She gave her art gallery that name because the building had formerly housed the bank, now out of business, in our tiny middle Georgia town. She was the counselor for the Youth Fellowship and my strongest supporter when I was in high school. She saw me through my senior year, got me ready to go to college, and inspired me in ways I hardly understood at the time. Though I didn't know the word then, she was my *mentor*.

Mentoring is a concept that is bandied about a lot these days. Google lists more than 50 million entries for mentoring! Like "family values" or "effective parenting," the definition depends on who's doing the defining. Basically, a mentor is an advisor and sounding board to someone less experienced; a wise and trusted teacher. The relationship between an experienced and a less experienced person can be formal or informal. The traditional model is that of an apprentice learning from a master. In formal mentoring, there are usually program goals, schedules, training (for mentors and mentees), and evaluations. Informal mentoring occurs organically, where we seek out a person who knows something we need to know, someone who is farther along the path and is willing to bring us along.

Good mentors teach us what we need to know. The difference between success and failure in almost all aspects of life is the presence of mentors. Mentors often pick up where "good-enough" parenting leaves off (more about that subject later). Short of a lightning strike, children with both good-enough parenting and good mentors will fulfill their destinies.

Unfortunately, not everyone can accept mentoring. Those who have not had supportive parents or parent surrogates as a backdrop often fend off mentors. Fragile, insecure, poorly nurtured children can feel insecure and defensive. They feel too overwhelmed and fearful to admit how little they know and how much support they need. Being a good mentee means being an eager student, being willing to learn and grow. My eighty-six-year-old friend has spent her life mentoring others—as a second-grade teacher for thirty years, as a church deacon, as a financial supporter of families seeking to educate their children, as an active participant in family and community affairs. At age eighty-five she began a *formal* study on mentoring. I was surprised to find her reading a book on the subject. "This broadens my world," she told me. Maybe it's as simple as that. We can be good mentors while at the same time being eager mentees.

My sharecropper parents, who never completed fifth grade, provided me with good-enough parenting, which made it easy for me to reach out to Mary Bradley, a college graduate and successful businesswoman. When she helped me get to college, I then was mentored by my freshman English teacher, Miss Munck, who took me under her wing. During the second semester of my freshman year, Miss Munck learned that I was considering dropping out of school for financial reasons. She called me into her office.

"Leen, I won't let you do that," she said. I was stunned by the authority and conviction I heard in her voice. "Don't make any decision until we talk again," she said, touching my shoulder and walking me to her door. Several days later I learned that she had arranged for a local church she attended to provide a scholarship for me. Four years later she was my "candle lighter" at an alumnae induction service. For more than forty years after my graduation, we kept in touch. In the years before her death severe dementia eventually claimed her mind and she couldn't remember. I can't forget.

We all have the potential for being good mentors. Sometimes we are a mentor without knowing it. Rites of initiation into adulthood involve adults promising to be mentors. Baptisms and first communions call on adults to promise to support and encourage the less experienced on their journey. Ceremonial rites of passage and accepted wisdom acknowledge that it takes a village to guide a child into adulthood. If we do not provide this guidance and support, if we do not mentor our young, they will get into trouble and be "mentored" by larger institutions such as gangs, prisons, mental hospitals.

There is a major difference between a mentor and an advisor. A mentor walks the walk with you. A mentor is a role model. Mary Bradley walked side by side with me and her role was critical. Without her presence at a pivotal time in my life, I might still be in my rural Georgia hometown packing peaches.

Well into her late eighties, Mary Bradley has stayed in touch—a mentorship of more than fifty years. She still wants to know what I'm doing. She reads my books, and as an artist provided illustrations for one of them. Recently I visited her in the hospital near her home in the mountains of north Georgia. I sat on her bed and held her hand as I told her what she had meant to me.

"Oh, Leen, I don't think I did that much," she whispered. "All I did was love you." I brushed back a tear.

"Rumor has it, that's enough," I said.

2

Outside the Window

AS A CHILD, I WAS EAGER TO RUN to my friend's house and call through the screen door, "Can you come out and play?" For as long as I can remember, I have known that the fragrance of peach blossoms, the glow of fireflies, the sounds of frogs and crickets in the humid summer all made me feel good. As an adult, I have come to appreciate more and more the value of being in touch with nature and its healing potential.

In my clinical practice, I often see nature work its magic. "When my son almost lost his life in an automobile accident while he was driving drunk, I did not want to live," one client said. "I kept thinking, 'I can't do this again. I survived being the daughter of alcoholic parents, but this is too much to bear.'" Her eyes filled with tears.

"Yet here you are," I said. "What has changed?"

She brightened. "Well, shortly after the accident, I was sitting staring out the window, looking into my back yard. My eyes fell on a beautiful tree I had planted there eighteen years ago, when my son was a tiny child. I sat staring at the tree and the thought came to me that even while I was asleep, that tree grew."

My client had seen, in nature, a fresh hope in her own life. "I had planted it, but I didn't have to do anything to *make* it grow. A natural process was going on while I was sleeping. The tree didn't *try* to be a tree. It just *was*. I didn't have to *try* to be a mother. I just *was*. This awareness lifted a cloud of gloom and guilt, and helped me cast my hope in a new direction. I was no longer rooted exclusively in my earthly family. I was rooted in something more solid and dependable. It sounds strange, I know, but suddenly, I didn't feel completely hopeless."

I did not find my client's experience strange. Nature—the outdoors—is a powerful healer. We all seek "a room with a view." Family vacations often focus on the mountains or the ocean. In the business world, status is partly defined in terms of who gets the office with a window.

Nature extends an invitation to us to rest, as well as to experience joy and awe. We can do with the invitation whatever we choose. We can respond in love, gratitude, and appreciation for our place in the natural order, or, we can ignore our place and act as though we are the center of the universe. Nature is the source of true humility. One of its lessons is the simplicity of its call.

In her collection of essays *Coastal Notes*, psychiatrist and author Catherine McCall says, "Nature is our oldest teacher. From the reliability and resilience of the daily sunrise, to the cyclical transformation of the seasons, the living earth offers a cornucopia of lessons. Its drama is our daily gift, its beauty our daily grace."

I believe that observing nature is the path to wisdom. We learn from ancient Chinese tradition that being truly connected to nature is being "in Tao." Awareness of our place in nature gives life proportion and meaning. It takes us outside ourselves and gives us a universal perspective.

As a psychotherapist for more than forty years, I have come to understand that a broken life requires a perspective of something greater than self. Without that perspective, we are at risk for symptoms of poor adjustment: depression, anxiety, fear, isolation, despair. It matters whether our take on existence is that we are totally isolated, alone with our pain—or that as one cell in the organism of life, we are connected.

It is not surprising that many forms of meditation include observing nature's beauty and awesomeness. Such meditation springs spontaneously from a deep human need. It is that moment when we stop to consider meaning, causes, and consequences. When we listen to the calm ocean and contemplate the constant, predictable movement of the tides, when we stare in awe at the foot of a snow-capped mountain, or hike a trail at the peak of fall foliage, we can step outside the drama of our particular circumstances and know that the forces at work in nature go on without our effort. "Relax," say the rocks and hills and rivers. "Don't work so hard, little person; you won't be here long. Enjoy!" We are without excuse in tapping into this healing source, because everywhere nature proclaims this truth.

Where do we find our strength? The Hebrew psalmist said, "I will lift up mine eyes unto the hills. . . ." Siddhartha, who later became the Buddha, gained enlightenment as he sat by the river and watched the flow of water. Rumi, the thirteenth-century Persian poet, wrote: "The body is a device to calculate the astronomy of the spirit. . . . This is wisdom: to remember the original clay and not get drunk with ego and arrogance."

A client who was struggling with family upheaval and pain reported a recurring dream of windows. In the dream, she told herself she couldn't stop to look out a window because she was lost and had to find her way home. My suggestion to her was that she pay attention to her dream. I encouraged her to stop her frantic rushing around, pull up a comfortable chair and look out her window, quietly noting what she observed, and record her thoughts. Later, she told me that this exercise had helped her get a broader perspective—a different "view" of things. I believe that each of us needs to spend more time looking out windows, bearing witness to the beauty and wonder of nature and embracing its restorative powers.

3

Gracelets

It was one of Miss Molly's favorite words, and I was never sure if it was a real word or if Miss Molly made it up to describe something too special for ordinary words to convey.

Gracelets, according to Miss Molly, were very special people who came into your life when you least expected them and showered their presence on you like tiny sparkling drops of morning dew. Gracelets were special people who taught important lessons about life and how to live it.

Miss Molly was in her eighties when I was in high school, a widowed black woman who earned her livelihood ironing for "rich white folk." She lived alone just outside of town in a run-down shanty without running water or electricity, and used an old-fashioned flatiron rather than the modern steam kind. I loved spending winter afternoons sitting on the floor by the ironing board, watching her. She lifted the heavy black iron she had heated in front of the open fire, wiped it on a damp cloth, then gracefully pushed it over each starched white shirt and lovely cotton dress. Her hand was twisted with arthritis and missing a finger she told me she'd lost in childhood when she had tried to split firewood with a hatchet and missed.

"You goin' to meet lots of folks who will be gracelets for you when you get grown and leave this place," Miss Molly told me. "You're gonna meet lots and lots of important people and they goin' to teach you good lessons about life and make you think about things in ways you can't imagine. Just you wait and see, now."

My first such encounter with a famous person came my freshman year in college when anthropologist Margaret Mead spoke on campus and held small group discussions. She answered every question, no matter how naive, with patience and good humor.

The lesson I learned from Dr. Mead that day was from her response to a student's question about doing volunteer work in other countries. With the straightest of faces she replied, "The basic problem with do-gooders," she said, "is that they often forget to ask the do-good-ees how they want to be done good to." While this was a casual comment that generated laughter among her young listeners, it was profound. It shaped my approach to counseling. Instead of assuming that I know what my clients want and need, I always ask, "What can I do to help?" "What do you need from me?" "How can I help make things better for you?"

To me, Margaret Mead was a gracelet. So was Eleanor Roosevelt, another famous figure, who agreed to meet with eighteen selected college students from around the country in her New York home, in the summer of 1957. I was among them. I couldn't believe that this was happening to me.

The chartered bus carried us from Manhattan to Hyde Park on a beautiful Sunday. We arrived at a long, narrow driveway, which the driver hesitated to enter, not knowing where he should park.

Almost immediately, a slightly disheveled older woman with a loose-fitting white shirt and an ankle-length cotton print skirt knocked on the door of the bus. We all assumed that the housekeeper had been sent to direct us, and stared in amazement when Mrs. Roosevelt stepped onto the bus, said a crisp "hello," and told the driver exactly where to park, as we proceeded down the dirt road.

We all sat on the front lawn, eating box lunches served by Mrs. Roosevelt. She took a seat in front of us in a wooden lawn chair, its white paint fading and chipping with age. For more than two hours she spoke with us about our lives and what we planned to do with them, about her work and her concerns for the poor and sick. She spoke about world affairs, and encouraged us all to be involved in important matters affecting humankind. I was spellbound, not only because I was in the presence of such a famous woman, but even more because of her humility, her unpretentiousness, her passion, and her sense of purpose.

Miss Molly was right.

When, in my late twenties, I met Lillian Smith, author of *Strange Fruit* and *Killers of the Dream,* I knew that she, too, was a gracelet according to Miss Molly's definition. She was speaking at a college in Atlanta, and two friends and I who had been moved by her writings drove up to hear her.

There was a quality in the work of Lillian Smith that I had long ago found compelling. She was passionate. She felt the pain of racial segregation and wrote about the demoralizing and demeaning effect it had on *all* of us, in a way few people could. She continued her writing and speaking despite threats to her life and the burning of her north Georgia home. The courage and compassion she portrayed, and the risks she took in order to point us toward a better future, remain forever vivid in my mind.

The late Walter Russell is another of the gracelets in my life, not because I knew Russell personally but because I have been so inspired by the account of his extraordinary life as sculptor, musician, architect, and philosopher. Glenn Clark's slim volume *The Man Who Tapped the Secrets of the Universe* records Russell's story. When I read Russell's words of wisdom I feel a special kinship with him, as though he is telling my story with his words—reinforcing my ability to trust my own experiences. I often give this little book to others as a way of sharing what I have gained from it.

I now understand that we receive gracelets from many sources. People come into our lives at critical moments to give us encouragement and support, set us on a new path, hold up a mirror for us to see our true selves. Not only the famous, but unknown, uncredentialed, ordinary people—each with a special gift to give us, an indelible mark to make on our hearts, footprints to leave on our souls. In my young life, Miss Molly had herself been one of my gracelets. By the time I came to understand that, it was too late to thank her, but I made her a solemn promise that I would always be on the lookout for more.

4

Tilling the Soul

"MY BEANS NEED PICKING," SAID MA BAREFOOT as she instructed me to "jar up" some leftover food to take home. "But I can't work out in the garden alone now. I'm afraid I'll fall and those fire ants could destroy me before anyone could find me."

"I'll come on Saturday morning and help you," I said. Ma Barefoot, of course, was not *my* mother; she was a fixture in our community, a mother of sorts to all. Her husband, Pop, equally loved by everyone, had died eight years earlier. Ma was left to run the household by herself now. She started before light, came into the house in the heat of the day, and worked into the night from early spring to first frost, tending an acre of rotating crops—all by hand. She carried jugs up and down the rows to provide water, and turned the soil with a rusty old push plow. She talked to the bees and mosquitoes to keep from being bitten, but she was not as persuasive with encroaching deer and fire ants.

"What time do you get up?" she asked me.

"Tell me when you want me here," I said. "Seven? Seven-thirty?"

"Be here at six. By eight o'clock you have to quit because it's too hot."

On Saturday I rolled out of bed at five-fifteen, made coffee, and headed to Ma's. We were in the field by six-thirty, held up half an hour by an unexpected thunder shower. I wore jeans and a T-shirt and old sneakers. Ma headed out the back door barefoot and stopped to put on tennis shoes with holes in the top. We each took a three-gallon bucket and put a wheelbarrow near the end of our row to empty the buckets into. The garden had rows of corn, cucumbers, squash, and string beans.

"I worked out here yesterday while my friend mowed grass," she said, bending over the first row. "All we need to do is pick the beans."

Piece of cake, I thought. *How long can this take*? We stood on either side of a long row that seemed to be half bean plants and half corn stalks.

I tackled my side of the row with confidence as Ma picked opposite me on the other side. We moved from plant to plant, each more heavily laden than the one before. Sweat beaded up on my forehead and ran down my nose, taking flying leaps into the bucket of beans. Ma, too, was sweating in no time. Within fifteen minutes we had our buckets filled. Ma instructed me to carry them back to the wheelbarrow and dump them in.

"Move over to the next row, so them fire ants won't get you," she shouted after me as I carried the heavy buckets.

I quickly jumped over the cucumber plants to a safer trail to the wheelbarrow. I was relieved to see that we were approaching the first corn stalk—which I was thinking of as the finish line. But as we got closer, it became apparent that our work was just beginning. More beans were planted *between* the stalks, and the row went on forever!

Ma continued to talk amiably as she picked the vegetables. "The garden has always been my joy. Before Pop died we worked in it together. I have pushed a plow all over this garden. Don't you think Pop is proud of my crop?" It was more of a statement than a question. "I believe he sees all this; I feel him with me all the time." I headed back to the wheelbarrow, laden with two buckets of beautiful beans. The end of the row was in sight.

"When we finish this row, we only have a half row left," Ma said as I returned with the empty buckets. "That's when you're thankful you only planted half a row instead of another full one," she said with a smile.

We asked each other every few minutes how the other was doing, and the answer was always the same: "Fine." But the sun was beating down, and Ma watched as I made the third trip to the wheelbarrow. Sweat was dripping off our faces, my T-shirt was stuck to my body, and my jeans felt heavy with water and dirt.

"I thought, 'O, Lordy, you're going to die,' when you stood up that last time," Ma said. "I heard your heavy breathing."

I didn't say so, but I considered it a minor miracle that I was breathing at all. We were almost finished with the beans. I have never seen myself as particularly competitive, and my higher self would like to think that I wasn't hanging in there just to keep an eighty-three-year-old from showing me up. But we all have our shallow places.

After I had emptied the last bucket of beans, we started back to the house. Ma announced that now we could pick the squash and cucumbers in the row we would be walking down. Bean buckets became summer squash and cucumber buckets. I wondered how she could ever use all those beans. My answer came right away.

Ma kicked off her muddy shoes and invited me into the house. "Dial this number for me," she said, and I dialed the phone and handed it to her. "Do you want some fresh beans?" she said to someone on the other end of the line. "Luleen and me have picked beans and we're going to bring you some." She put the phone back in its cradle.

"That's my ninety-seven-year-old friend Miss Billie," Ma said. "She's blind and she loves fresh beans. And we'll take a bag to my friend Lila. She's had surgery and she fell yesterday but we're rejoicing that she was able to get up. Get four of those store bags and we'll fill them up. You take two for yourself. We'll take one to Lila and one to Miss Billie."

We filled up the bags and I put them in the car. Ma climbed in and directed me to Miss Billie's home. I waited in the car as my tiny friend with her small bare feet climbed the back steps and handed the bag to an elderly woman who opened the door.

"I didn't call Lila 'cause she might still be asleep," Ma explained to me at the next stop. "We'll just leave her beans at her back door." We did. "This is such a joy to me," Ma said. Her eyes sparkled and danced as she climbed back in the car, and we left unnoticed.

"Two friends are coming this afternoon to put plants in my barrels in the front yard," Ma told me. "They'll plant flowers and I'll feed them. I'll give Olive some beans, and I'll see if Chuck and Charlene want some when they come to see me this afternoon."

I parked the car in Ma's driveway, and we returned to the wheelbarrow and poured two buckets of water over the remaining beans. Then we scooped them into a bucket with holes in the bottom and set them on the back steps to dry. Ma was radiant. At that moment I realized that by her daily actions she defines the concept of community. She is loved and appreciated and treasured, and she gives love and veggies in return.

It was time for me to go.

"I wish I could tell you the joy it gave me to have you on the other side of that row, picking those beans with me," she said. "Don't die, now; they'll need picking again in a couple of weeks."

I nodded and gave her a thumbs-up as I drove away, tired but exhilarated. As is often the case when I am in Ma's presence, something magical had happened. I came to understand that this experience wasn't about picking beans in the early morning light; not about tilling the soil. It was about sharing and nurturing. It was about tilling the soul.

5

Learn from Suffering

If you are alive, you either *have* suffered, *are* suffering, or *will* suffer. We all live under the shadow of suffering and death. Given this truth, how can we find happiness in and through suffering? How can we stop viewing suffering as an enemy or obstacle and instead see it as a potential ally or partner? The first step is to accept that we will suffer, then prepare ourselves as best we can for it, and when it comes, ask ourselves what it has to teach us—what we can learn through the experience that contributes to happiness.

Happiness that emerges out of adversity has a profound, enduring quality, not only because it requires a level of personal maturity and wisdom, but also because the experience itself increases our capacity to endure suffering. Eleanor Roosevelt said, "We gain strength, courage, and confidence by every experience in which you really stop to look fear in the face. You must do the thing which you think you cannot do."

On the other hand, suffering in and of itself—whether physical or psychological—does not guarantee happiness. Pain can be so strong, so intense, that the individual can break under it. We don't have to understand why this happens, but we do need to accept it and not judge ourselves or others who are unable to bear the burden.

"I thought I was going to die when my husband put a gun to my head," my client said. "Instead, the next thing I knew I was lying in a pool of blood, my head smashed on the bathroom floor." For years, this woman has dealt with the physical and psychological effects of that attack and other beatings. Today she is in an important position in the domestic violence field, helping hundreds of women and children deal with abusive relationships and start a new life. "I'm very effective at what I do," she told me. "And it's absolutely clear to me that my suffering had a purpose."

People who are suffering often look for someone to blame. The usual suspects:

God: "Why me? What have I done to deserve this? Is God punishing me? I've lost my faith—I don't believe in God anymore."

Self: "Maybe I'm a bad person—I do feel guilty all the time. Maybe I'm not a worthy person." Often suicidal clients say they don't deserve to live. "I caused this; I'm to blame." "Why am I the only one feeling this way and dealing so badly with this? Everybody else has problems and they deal with them fine. In fact, I should be able to handle this without help."

"Find somebody and blame them"—we know that feeling. The Jews are to blame. Blacks are to blame. Queers are to blame. Illegal immigrants are to blame. No? Then God or I must be. No? Then who? Just tell me so I can make them pay!

A favorite cartoon of mine makes this point. The husband insists: "You can't blame me for that!" The wife replies: "You obviously underestimate my talent for blaming."

To get beyond blame is an important step in finding acceptance and happiness. Another challenge is to resist the natural temptation to avoid or deny pain. A client of mine came in a few weeks after her aged mother died in an Alzheimer's facility. "How are you doing?" I asked with great concern.

"I'm okay," she said, her face in a deep scowl. "I'm fine."

"Really?" I asked. "You don't look fine."

After a brief silence, my client began to sob. "Handling my mother's estate is driving me to drink. I'm furious with my husband and I'm thinking about a divorce." She had tried to dodge the very feelings that nature provides for growth and healing. Bringing these feelings into the open allowed for healing to begin.

Suffering brings us the opportunity to grow and to change. It also gives us the opportunity to become bitter and miserable. The choice is always there. A close friend recently went through cancer surgery. "I tried to remain optimistic and get through what I needed to do," she told me. "When you come right down to it, the only other choice is to whine and rant and complain, and I can't function that way." Her surgery was successful and she is cancer free. I asked her how the suffering had changed her.

"I feel a certain sense of triumph that I did handle things with some degree of dignity," she replied. "In addition, I now take so much pleasure in such simple things. It doesn't seem to take much to make me happy. Likewise, what was important to me before—getting recognition, being in the spotlight, always being right—doesn't matter to me now. I really believe that my illness enriched my quality of life."

The capacity to love is often enhanced as a result of such a trauma. Suffering can make us more sensitive to others and teach us to put forth a greater love for everything. What is essential is whether we take an active part in the process. If we do, the act of suffering is then a project—a condition to learn about and discuss with others who have had similar experiences, so that we become able to exert some control in the situation.

We can transform our attitudes and ways of thinking. Holocaust survivor Victor Frankl, author of *Man's Search for Meaning,* says that the one freedom that cannot be taken away is the ability to choose our attitude in any given situation. Philosopher Friedrich Nietzsche said, "He who has a *why* to live for, can bear with almost any how."

While suffering is unavoidable, we should not seek it out. We do not get extra points for gratuitous suffering. Nor does all pain and suffering have to be accepted and endured. If we can help diminish suffering, ours or that of another, we are called upon to do that.

"Will there come a time when I won't recognize my wife?" asked my Alzheimer's client who had been married for more than fifty years.

"Probably so," I answered. "But for now you do recognize her and you can call her by name every day and tell her how much you love her. If you do that, I believe that when the time comes that you don't recognize her, it will be all right."

We do not fully understand suffering. We don't have to, so long as we accept that suffering is a natural part of living and has something to teach us. A few years ago I stepped off a sidewalk, took a bad spill, and broke my ankle in three places, requiring major surgery and months of rehabilitation. Pain was a constant companion for a long time. In accepting this circumstance, in participating in the treatment plan, in reaching out for support, I came to see what lesson I needed to learn from the experience. The issue for me had to do with balance, both literal and symbolic. By seeing the accident as a metaphor for my life, I came to accept that I was getting too old to continue to work full-time, that it was time for me to retire. The time at home in a wheelchair allowed me to develop a workable plan: to give up my office, work from my home, and wind down my clinical practice.

Making this decision, which I had postponed for a long time, had an immediate healing, liberating effect. I took joy in sleeping late, in traveling, and in having time and freed-up creative energy to write a book. At the time of my injury my closest friends came together as a team and shared responsibility for my care during the recovery. Out of this collaboration has come a solid bond of deep friendships, not only for me, but for each of them. At my retirement party, one of them said to those gathered, "Leen stepped off a curb and into another world." She was right. As Victor Frankl also said, "What is to give light must endure the burning."

6

The Voluntary Life

"AT MY AGE I'M SURPRISED EACH DAY when I wake up alive," my almost-ninety-year-old friend said to me. "I open my eyes and volunteer to live another wonderful day." My elderly friend is very wise. We who know and love him enjoy his days, too! Even though his physical strength is lessening, he infects me with his enthusiasm and optimism every time I see him.

I often write while in Isla Mujeres, Mexico, a tiny island in the Gulf of Mexico off Cancun that has become my second home. Here I am struck by the openness, helpfulness, and humor among the people, especially in the Mayan culture. I am inspired by their love of community and grateful for my connection to the natural beauty of this way of life.

Earlier today I read on the wall of a nature preserve a quote from the Mayan sacred text, Popol Vuh: "He who withers flowers will inherit the bitterness of his grandchildren's children."

"Yikes!" my companion said as I read the quote to her. "That sounds like a heavy price to pay for flowers!"

But to me it is not a threat; it is not just about causing a flower to wither.

This quote got my attention because it is about *me*. The flower I don't want to wither is the flower of my own life. My friend and I talked about this.

"I know what it feels like to be withered," she said. "When I'm withered, everything I touch is in danger of withering. And when I am blossoming, everyone I come in contact with is better off." So it really matters who and what we surround ourselves with. Conversely, it matters to everyone around us what kind of mood we are in.

The power of feng shui, the ancient Chinese practice of placement and arrangement of space to achieve harmony with the environment, is similar to the flower illustration. The purpose of this three-thousand-year-old practice is to arrange our environment to enhance the quality of our lives—in other words, to improve the balance of natural elements externally so that the inner life will reflect better balance.

A mother knew her daughter was lonely and going from superficial trysts to lousy boyfriends. As the daughter began her professional life, her clever mother suggested she purchase several things for her new apartment. For her front porch she bought a sculptured family of frogs and a blooming plant. For her office, she found a framed print of stylized dancers in a pas de deux; for her bedroom, a petite print wall hanging with pairs of birds worked into the pattern in her daughter's favorite colors. After these changes were made in her daughter's life according to feng shui principles, by happy coincidence her daughter met her soul mate, whom she eventually married.

Choices matter. Change the outer environment and the inner life changes in the same direction. Change inner beliefs and attitudes, and the outer world and the people around you will change in similar ways. One of my friends has a sign on her refrigerator which reads, "The world is constantly rearranging itself to accommodate to my perception of it."

In my professional life and in other arenas, I have seen many withered lives and witnessed the harvest of bitterness. However, I have also seen that no situation is hopeless and that a family's life can improve if just one family member begins to bloom. There may be practical problems to solve: matters of the heart, finances, career choices. Proper medications and therapies may be helpful, but sometimes people are so deeply attached to their misery that traditional treatments do not seem to work.

I know of a resourceful and wise psychologist who told his "withered" client to go home and plant a flower in a pot. When the flower blossomed, he instructed his client to give it to somebody and root another plant. Slowly the client's depression lifted and he had a beautiful garden growing. The act of planting flowers translated into reality the change the therapist wished for his client. When the inner life is withered, the environment suffers. Starting with the outer life can help the inner. This may account for the psychological basis of the Chinese belief in feng shui. It works.

There is a biblical story of a person sowing seeds. Some seeds fall on fertile ground, some on barren, rocky soil. The story may be a parable about the responsibility of the receiver to be prepared to receive the gifts that come along—to provide fertile ground. I believe that it is also helpful to look at the generosity of the sower. I love the image of sheer joy and reckless abandon in this character. I like to imagine the sower as a woman with arms outstretched, lovingly tossing seeds without thought of where they will fall. I think of her as free from preconceived notions about which soil is more worthy or judgments about what will bring the biggest return on her investment. She just did her part.

Sometimes we talk about giving of ourselves in formal ways. We put much structure around the activity, and less emphasis on the motivation for, or the spirit of, our giving. We make arrangements for our children to experience the feeling of doing something for someone in need because we know how important it is. All of us have participated in some acts—formal and informal—in which we have sought to be of help to others. And we are the better for it. Having this commitment is important, especially when calamities strike. Hurricanes, tsunamis, tornadoes, landslides, and coal-mine tragedies remind us that there is always something we can, and should, do to help.

To me, making this commitment reflects an attitude about myself and my neighbors. It's opening my heart up so I can be in a relationship with life in a way that benefits us all. It's who I am. If I get beyond identifying and labeling each *act*, I get to the heart of this concept, which allows me to live life to the fullest. I choose to smile at a child; to take delight in the butterfly on my hibiscus; to express joy and appreciation for my friend's thoughtful gesture; to offer a shoulder to a loved one. I make a decision to express my gratitude for life itself. I decide to love and to be loved. I make a commitment to be. I volunteer.

The usual definition of a volunteer as "one who works without being paid" is at least a start, and is important. It is healthy and curative for us to get beyond our material self-interest and to think more of others. It's never too late to begin living the voluntary life. Yet, lifting this concept to its highest level is to see all our actions with others as a love connection. If my love connection to life is as an artist, I might naturally volunteer at a museum or teach a neighbor's child to use watercolors. If my love connection is gardening, I might give of my time and resources to an arboretum or join the Nature Conservancy. Whether it flows from within, or is taught to us by those older or wiser, the voluntary life is a generative life.

Pure selflessness may not only be difficult or impossible, but may actually not be desirable. If the flowers matter, if the suffering of others matters, it is because *I also matter*. Everyone benefits. The spirit of deep connectedness naturally leads to genuine care and generosity. It is selfless *being* that produces a way of life guaranteeing that neither we nor the fellow travelers on our journey will experience the harvest of bitterness. Who wouldn't want to volunteer for this?

lesson two

The Knack of Being Happy with Yourself

You carry
All the ingredients
To turn your life into a nightmare—
Don't mix them!
. . .
You carry all the ingredients
To turn your existence into joy,
Mix them, mix
Them!

—HAFIZ

Being happy with self is a challenge throughout life, and is always a challenge. There are three essentials for building self-esteem at each stage of life: an accurate assessment of our strengths and weaknesses, the ability to be content with who we are, and the expectation of continuing personal growth. Our task is the mastery of issues at each age; otherwise we are trapped in old "stuff." If we have mastered the developmental issues of our twenties, we draw courage as we face our unknown thirties.

Life is not about competition. It is not a contest to see who wins, who is right, who is best. We all come in first! No one is second.

7

The Power to Choose

"I FOUND THIS FEATHER AND I WANTED to bring it to you, but Michael said you wouldn't like it," my three-year-old son said, many years ago now, tears rolling down his cheeks. I gave him a hug and dried his eyes. "Well, Michael doesn't know everything," I said.

"I know; only me!" my son said with a big smile. The three-year-old who has the confidence of his, or her, own knowledge will carry that confidence into later life.

Self-esteem building begins at a very early age. It is part of the backdrop of a child's search for identity and for self-respect. As parents we have a responsibility to look for ways to build a solid sense of self in our children. One of the best ways to build a healthy, *realistic* feeling of self-worth is to help children develop skills for judicious self-evaluation. Many parents fear that if they build up their child too much they will create selfish little monsters. While I suppose that is possible, in my sixteen years of dealing with children as coordinator of psychological services in a large school system, as well as dozens of years spent with children and adolescents in private clinical practice, I have yet to see a child suffering from too much self-esteem.

The selfish monsters I've run into had too little, not too much. Conceit or narcissism, yes, but not too much self-esteem.

"Self-esteem" comes from the root word "to estimate." It involves a *realistic* appraisal of our strengths and weakness, allowing us to draw the conclusion that we are competent in some important areas and lacking in others. One of my favorite wise old women friends is fond of saying, "We're not born knowing everything. I'm just like everybody else. Why act surprised if I don't know something? Every day I broaden my world."

The knack of self-esteem is an *accurate* self-assessment. I have some control, some individuality, some skills, some fun, some things to learn. I'm just one little person—but I *am* a person and my life matters to me. My own individual, authentic self matters to me! Our ultimate goal is that children learn to value not only themselves, but all other selves.

Teaching coping skills to children increases their sense of mastery and self-worth, and makes them feel less vulnerable. Mastery and coping skills allow children to feel that they have some control over a range of situations. Children who feel that *the locus of control is inside themselves* feel more secure and confident than those who feel they are totally helpless and powerless and that the locus of control—the deciding or controlling factor or circumstance—is *always* outside themselves. The smart mother does not ask her child, "Do you want an egg for breakfast?" if she wants the child to eat an egg. Instead she says, "Do you want your egg scrambled, fried, or boiled this morning?" The child then has the esteem-building power to decide.

While we as parents often have to make big decisions for our children, we can allow them control over what color sneakers they want to buy, or what pair of shorts they want to wear. Children need to learn early that their thoughts, opinions, and actions matter. For good or ill, there are consequences. Smile and the world smiles back. Bite people, hit, fight, bully, have tantrums—and you'll be alone and not too happy.

Jodie was fourteen when she was referred to me by her school counselor. A pretty, petite brunette with dark brown eyes, she plopped herself into my overstuffed chair, curled her feet up, and began a tirade about not being able to talk to her mother about anything important. Her mother refused to let her sleep over at a friend's house; she insisted that she accompany Jodie to the hair stylist, instructing the stylist as to the cut she wanted her daughter to have. Ditto for shopping and clothes buying.

"Your mother doesn't seem to value your opinions," I said.

"My mother's position is, 'When you have an opinion, I'll tell you,'" Jodie responded.

We agreed that I would meet with her mother and then with the two of them together to see if her mother could let go of some of the control and thereby give her child support for learning how to make good decisions.

A few weeks later Jodie stuck her head in my office. "I love your new haircut," I said to her.

"Thanks! Mom stayed home and I got to go alone and choose what I wanted. She's relieved that I didn't come back with a Mohawk! Things are working out."

Children can come to know that they can master their own fate early in life. "Fiona wants to hold my hand and tries to kiss me when we walk to school," my son confided to me the first week of kindergarten.

"If you don't want her to do that, you can just tell her that right now you don't like to be kissed by girls or have your hand held when you're on your way to school," I assured him. "If she doesn't understand that, I'll talk with her mother." He seemed relieved.

"Okay. Actually, right now I only like one girl and she's a grown-up lady. Do you want to know who that is?"

"I'm kind of hoping that it's me," I said.

"Well, it is," my son said, proud of his ability to settle his own dilemma.

"But I only want one kiss a day from you, and I'll tell you when." Control over such minute matters translates into confidence in bigger ones!

Our goal in teaching locus of control and mastery is to have our children feel a sense of ownership in their behavior. Children who believe that nothing they say or do has any power may harbor the seeds of helplessness and victimization, and compensatory feelings of rage and vengeance.

As we grow older, these questions are not always as simple as who kisses and gets kissed. For adolescents and adults alike, there's a fine line between homicide and suicide. A person who wishes she or he were different—taller, richer, smarter, thinner—is in serious danger of being very critical of, and damaging to, self and others. Poor relationships result on all sides.

"I can't stand my mother's bossiness," says one teenager. "I can't stand my husband's constant criticism," says a frustrated wife. "I can't stand my children's back talk." These are all attitude problems flowing from the subject of the sentence. It is *I* who must change. I must call time out. Any amount of time is not too much to devote to accepting who I am, who I am created to be. No effort is too great in learning not to blame others, but to get on with *my* life.

8

Getting beyond the Looking Glass

"LEEN, YOU AREN'T GOING TO BELIEVE IT!" my fifteen-year-old-friend said, obviously upset. "Grandma actually told me she was hoping I wouldn't have big breasts like my mother!" My young friend began to cry. "Why couldn't she criticize something about me I could change—not my cup size! Wouldn't you think she'd know that I don't like my big boobs either?"

A few days later, a forty-year-old client told me about her estranged father's recent death and announced that the small inheritance he had left her was going to pay for breast enhancement—something she had always wanted and could never afford. "He used to make me cry by making fun of my flat chest, so now he can pay for my boob job!"

Body image issues, like death and taxes, are always with us. How we perceive our bodies may have nothing to do with our actual appearance. And our perception almost always errs on the side of being too critical.

A distorted body image can lead to self-destructive behavior, like extreme dieting or binge eating. Becky, an adolescent client, so disliked the image she saw in the mirror over her dresser that she covered her reflection in brown paper. An anorexic, she ate one half of a fried egg for lunch and the other half for dinner. Along with four string beans, this was her daily diet.

Very few women are totally satisfied with their bodies. One of the most attractive older women I know dresses as though she just stepped out of a fashion magazine. She told me recently that although she has arthritis, she is unwilling to participate in a water aerobics class designed to help with the severe pain she experiences, because she refuses to wear a bathing suit, or even shorts, in public. Why? She doesn't want anyone to see her legs. She chooses instead to endure the pain.

Even movie stars are quick to point out some perceived defect. And Oprah Winfrey, one of the most powerful and wealthy women in the world, has shared with her fans her long struggle with weight gain.

Some young women use thinness as a weapon, as a status symbol—"If I'm thin enough I'm better than anyone else." Ambitious, rigidly disciplined young women often seem to be especially susceptible to this desire for superiority and control. Being thin carries star power—"If I'm thin I'm the envy of everyone." Men have encouraged this view in contemporary society and have bought into the cultural fad of thinness.

The irony is that while we seem obsessed with thin, we Americans are an obese society. This is the boomerang effect of obsessions. The thing we fear comes upon us. When we obsess about food, regardless whether we overeat or undereat, food will be a constant issue.

Not all concern for our bodies is unjustified, of course. Changing something about the body that has lowered our self-esteem and caused pain or embarrassment doesn't mean that there is something wrong with us. Changing one's body image is not a moral issue; it is a health and practical issue. If there is something we *can* change that improves our feelings about ourselves we can evaluate the risks and benefits, the costs and promises, and make a healthy decision. Often it helps to check our body image with a trusted, honest friend to see if our perception seems accurate and our solution realistic and healthy. This is especially true when considering cosmetic surgery but applies as well to restorative dentistry, weight control procedures, dermatology, and skin treatments.

Men are not immune to an obsessive emphasis on physical appearance. The desire to fit the ideal masculine image—lean muscularity and rippled abs—can veer into overexercising and the use of dangerous and illegal drugs.

Thirty-five-year-old Dennis told me that ever since he was a young child he has been intensely angry at his parents because they did not opt for orthodontics to straighten his teeth. He blamed not having braces for his lack of success in a career, his dropping out of college, his divorce, and his abuse of alcohol.

"You're an adult now," I responded. "Why don't *you* get braces, if you're sure that's what's ruined your life?"

"Too late now," he said. He clung to his lame excuse rather than look squarely at his true self.

It's important that we not use a less-than-perfect appearance as a reason to blame someone else; it's also important that we not pin hopes for success and happiness exclusively, or unrealistically, on a body change. In our dealings with body image, we could benefit from the Serenity Prayer, which asks for courage to change what we can change, acceptance for what we cannot change, and wisdom to know the difference.

Physical appearance is more than teeth and muscles. Our bodies, our cars, our clothes, our houses all speak to how we view ourselves and how we judge others. I noticed a while back that my fourteen-year-old neighbor had become fixated on the cars people drive.

"Uncle Bill's pickup is all wrong for a lawyer," she said one day as I dropped her off at school. She amplified her case with other examples. "I wish Mama didn't have to drive that old Pontiac. Now, there's my car—a

Miata!" She glanced at the passing traffic again. "No, wait a minute, there's mine right there, a VW convertible." She was trying to match the meaning and value of a car with the meaning and value of a life.

Obsession with appearances puts a heavy burden on the young. Parents have a huge responsibility to be conscious of the impact their own words and attitudes have. To a great extent, the family and social milieu shapes the child's value system. As parents we need to be careful not to contribute to our children's concerns by thoughtless remarks, or by what we model about our own bodies. Parents might ask themselves how well they have adjusted to their own body image. Parents who have made peace with, and feel good about, the way their bodies look generally do not add critical burdens to their children.

The struggle with body image is universal. The way we handle it, however, is a clue to how we are handling life in general. The metaphorical advice I share with my clients is, "Accept the cards you were dealt, play the hand the best you can—but always keep in mind that you were not the dealer."

Negative body image develops over a lifetime and cannot be changed overnight. Peer pressure, growing up being teased about appearance, media images promoting thinness as the ideal, and a cultural tendency to judge people by their appearance—all these factors contribute to how we view ourselves. What can we do? We can try to untangle our body image from our childhood. We can talk with people who have similar concerns. And we can focus on health, and on physical activity for the fun of it. We can treat our body with respect. We can learn to relax and enjoy and appreciate this wonderful body that houses our spirit, and we can encourage those we love to join us.

9

What Are You Afraid Of?

I DID NOT WANT TO TELL MY BEST FRIEND that I had a lifelong phobia—a fear of drowning. I knew it was irrational, but this fear kept me from learning to swim or enjoying water sports. There was a kind of embarrassment, even shame, in admitting that although I had successfully treated many people with all kinds of anxiety disorders, I had never addressed my own.

Lucky for me, this particular phobia is not debilitating, and I lived a happy, successful life on dry land. Over the years I developed excuses for avoiding swimming. I forgot my bathing suit. I wasn't feeling well. I had to leave the pool party early. I'd rather take a long walk on the beach.

My friend and I were—not so long ago—at a quiet lagoon in Isla Mujeres, the tiny Mexican island that has become a haven for me in so many ways.

She wanted to give me a snorkeling lesson so I could share the magical underwater world she had discovered off the coast of the island. Her enthusiasm was contagious. I agreed. I wanted to believe that in this setting I could finally rid myself of my irrational fear. But as I put on my fins, my heart began to pound. As I dipped my mask in the water, my hands were shaking and I felt sick. Finally, the old fear was so intense that when I stood up, I carelessly skinned my knee, providing a face-saving excuse for why I couldn't possibly continue with the snorkeling lesson.

My friend had no idea of the turmoil going on inside me. Yes, I knew all about phobias, but knowing *about* it does not give mastery over it. Knowing about golf does not make you good at playing the game.

A phobia is a persistent, irrational fear of an object, situation, or activity that a person feels compelled to avoid. There are three classes of phobias. *Agoraphobia,* a "fear of the marketplace," is the most disabling, often turning sufferers into prisoners in their homes. For people with *social phobia,* work and social life are compromised. *Specific phobias* are among the most common and include fear of heights, water, flying, or driving, fear of speaking in public, and fear of animals. According to the National Institute of Mental Health, approximately 45 percent of the U.S. population suffers from one or more clinically significant phobias.

As a professional, I knew what caused phobias: a combination of genetic predisposition, combined with environmental and social events. Heredity, brain chemistry, emotional issues, abuse, and traumatic life experiences all can play a part in triggering phobias. When a client suffers from a phobia, my first step is to rule out any possible medical condition, then consider the stressors in their life and examine their coping methods. If this is not enough, anti-anxiety medications or, in some cases, anti-depressants, work well. For some, hypnosis is helpful.

I felt fortunate to know a local therapist who successfully treats phobias with EMDR (Eye Movement Desensitization and Reprocessing), a psychotherapeutic technique developed by Dr. Francine Shapiro. EMDR has proven exceptionally helpful to many people with phobias, traumas, and other problems associated with anxiety. This is the method I chose for confronting my phobia, after my friend, the snorkeler, found that EMDR removed her lifelong fear of social gatherings.

EMDR is especially effective with specific phobias deriving from trauma. One hypothesis is that in an extremely traumatic, highly charged emotional situation, the brain's usual competent method of processing information is overwhelmed. Thoughts, feelings, sounds, and images are jumbled together. Then, because the trauma is incompletely "processed," it gives rise to any number of symptoms. EMDR is said to somehow unbundle these elements, allowing a person to "reprocess" the sensory information and experience relief of symptoms.

In my case, what had not been completely processed were two very early traumatic events. One of my earliest memories, as the eighth child in a family of nine, is of standing in the middle of a goldfish pond in our yard screaming that I was drowning, even though the water level did not reach my knees. This episode coincided with the very significant loss of the older sister who had been my surrogate mother. As an abandoned three-year-old, I was "drowning" in tears.

Two years later I was hospitalized with diphtheria, a life-threatening bacterial disease that had killed an older brother. A thick membrane formed in my throat, making it hard to swallow or even breathe. This near-death experience became linked with the earlier experience of "drowning" in the goldfish pond, and a phobia was born.

One two-hour EMDR session allowed me to "unbundle" unconscious associations made between water/swimming and abandonment/death, and to become aware that my panic had nothing to do with swimming. For the first time I was free to look at swimming and water activities without fear or dread.

It's never too late to get rid of a phobia that is keeping you from doing something you want to do. I took my first swimming lesson on my sixty-eighth birthday, and two months later I went snorkeling off the coast of Mexico with my friend. The first excursion took us into water twenty feet deep. Two days afterward a boat took us to the second longest coral reef in the world, and there, along with my friend and twelve others, I donned my life jacket, fins, and snorkel and jumped into the turquoise blue Caribbean waters. A new world I had almost missed opened up right before my eyes.

With proper treatment, the vast majority of phobia sufferers can completely overcome their fears and live symptom-free. If you experience this kind of fear, the important thing to remember is that you are not alone. Phobias affect more than six million adult Americans. If fear is paralyzing you, or causing you to miss out on exciting adventures, help is available. Just don't develop a phobia about asking for it.

10

Risk a Revolution

I DID NOT FEEL LIKE A REVOLUTIONARY when, in August, 1961, I packed my little white Rambler sedan and prepared to leave my small Georgia hometown to drive to Boston. There I would begin a doctoral program in psychology at Boston University. On the back seat were my first and only record player, my two LP albums—*My Fair Lady* and *The Sound of Music,* two boxes of books, and a few small personal items. The trunk held my one suitcase and the few clothes I had.

"Come with me as far as New York City," I said to my niece Brenda, who had just graduated from high school in Atlanta. She had never been outside the state of Georgia, where she was born, and she was both excited and a little anxious. "You can help me drive, and we'll spend a couple of days in New York City seeing the sights. Then I'll put you on a plane back home. We'll count this as your graduation present."

"But, Leen, I've never been on a long trip, and I've certainly never been on an airplane."

"I know," I said. "Just trust me—it will be an adventure. You'll love it." I had helped teach my niece to drive a car, and she had obtained her learner's permit without any problem. Brenda packed her suitcase, squeezed it into the back of the car, and climbed in the passenger's seat. It was late August, and the air was already sticky as we pulled out of her driveway at seven a.m. Her mom—my sister—waved and blew kisses as we drove away.

With the air conditioner at full blast, we made small talk as I drove several hours before turning the wheel over to my former driving student. She slid under the wheel, then pulled out of the rest stop and onto the turnpike with confidence.

"Leen, what is that up ahead?" Brenda asked as she approached the first toll booth she had ever seen. She had been driving for an hour. I told her what it was.

"What am I going to do?" she asked.

"I hope you're going to stop," I said as I took money from my wallet.

"What if I don't stop in time?" she asked.

"Then I hope you know how to back up," I said with a smile.

"Wow! That was cool," Brenda said when she accomplished the task flawlessly, handing the toll over to the cashier and then merging easily into the flow of traffic on the other side of the booth. "Now can we find a bathroom?"

Later that afternoon, nearly an hour past our brief stop, Brenda suddenly began to cry.

"What's wrong?"

"I left my pocketbook back in that bathroom," she sobbed. "I just remembered." Luckily, we recalled the name of the place where we had stopped. I made a call, the pocketbook was found, and we retraced our steps back to get it.

"Are you hungry?" I asked as we resumed our trip with me in the driver's seat for a while. "We have to get gas, and we could get some supper, too."

I pulled into a glorified truck stop on the New Jersey Turnpike. We walked up to the counter to sit and grab a quick bite to eat, wanting to get into New York City as early in the evening as possible.

"Leen, there are two black men sitting at the counter," Brenda whispered. "What are you going to do?"

It had not registered with me that in her young life in the segregated South, my niece had never been faced with this situation. It constituted a dilemma for her.

"We're going to sit down and enjoy our food and hope that they enjoy theirs," I said as we took our seats beside one of the men. Nothing more was said as we ate our food and hit the road again. Once in Manhattan, we found the YWCA where I had reserved a room, and we dragged our weary bodies down the long hall. As we approached our room, an attractive young black woman came out of the room next to us. She was dressed in white shorts and T-shirt, and she carried a tennis racquet.

"Hi," Brenda said nonchalantly as I unlocked our door.

The young woman smiled. "Hi," she said. She looked at our luggage and said, "Here to see the sights?"

"Yes," Brenda said. "I can't wait."

"Enjoy," the woman called over her shoulder as she headed down the hallway.

After two days of sightseeing, I put Brenda on a plane back to Atlanta, where her parents would meet her. She was not the same frightened, ambivalent, anxious teenager who had begun the trip with her aunt.

I drove alone to Boston. On Commonwealth Avenue, looking for the entrance to the Boston University campus, I saw that I had passed right by it. I made a quick left turn, across trolley tracks, and heard a loud bell ringing and the sound of metal grinding against metal. I had narrowly escaped being hit by the MTA! The new and different world I had exposed my niece to was now mine. She and I were involved in a revolutionary process.

"Revolution" is "evolution" with an "r." We have only to look at nature to see that (r)evolution is a natural process. It is a process that inspires a certain amount of fear because nature is such a powerful force beyond our control. Sometimes we fail to give voice to our own internal revolutions. One definition of revolution is "far-reaching changes in ways of thinking and behaving." Leaving home is a revolutionary act. For me, leaving my roots to pursue a graduate degree from Boston University, to live and work in that area for almost three decades, was a personal revolution. The benefit of revolution is undeniable, but it can be scary and it can come with a high price.

If we think of a revolving door as a metaphor for our moving around a fixed point, we realize that timing is everything. We have to know when to go in, and, in order not to get stuck, when to get out. My niece could not stay in Manhattan alone. She had to return to her home. But she returned with a new sense of her own independence and more important, of our *inter*dependence. Today she shares this story with her grandchildren.

After thirty years, I needed to exit the revolving door in Boston, refocus my life, and move to coastal North Carolina. Along the way I learned that only the truly independent person can embrace interdependence, allowing herself to take part in life without needing to be the central character in a drama.

Self-awareness grows from being open to new places and people. It's revolutionary—it turns our lives upside down. Say *yes.* There is risk involved. Changes can be difficult. Say yes. Disaster can strike. Say yes. Keep saying yes to life.

Many years ago, a milk commercial touched on a profound truth as it proclaimed, "There's a new you coming every day!" After my globe-trotting friend Sally retired and moved back to her small hometown, I found her in her back yard, lying in her white cotton hammock stretched between two tall shade trees. I admired her tan and overall healthy glow as I teased her about her life of leisure. Sally smiled and said, "At the cellular level, I'm really quite busy!" She was right. At our deepest levels (r)evolutions are always occurring.

11

Lighten Up!

"DRIVING INTO NEW YORK CITY on a traffic-packed evening, my husband *had* to find the shortest line at the tunnel toll gate," Linda said. "He persisted in moving from line to line, risking other people's road rage—and sometimes mine—until finally he was sure he had found *the* shortest line. Only then was he happy."

Of the many personality profiles, one of the best known is the so-called type A personality, a term coined in the 1970s by Dr. Meyer Friedman and Dr. Ray Rosenman to describe the way some people approach life: the strict, rigid, uptight, perfectionistic, extremely ambitious individual.

Type A's are described as having significant problems with time: they need to be on time; they need to avoid running out of time. They are constantly experiencing a sense of *time urgency*. They eat fast and leave the dinner table immediately. They get upset standing in line in the grocery store or waiting to be seated in a restaurant. They become easily irritated and hostile when driving, and they swear at other drivers.

My type A friend Dena tells me: "One of the joys of dial-up computer service is that it takes a little time. So, in the morning I get out of bed, hit the computer dial-up button, go downstairs, hit the coffee-maker button, feed the cats, get a cup of freshly brewed coffee, run back upstairs, sit down at the computer, and have a contest to see how many things I can organize on my desk while waiting for the Internet connection. Time is crucial."

Another type A friend, Maggie, explained to me, "Planning my day to make the most efficient use of time means drawing up a plan the night before. Like tomorrow: I will drive to the dentist's office to return a magazine I borrowed, renew my membership at the art museum two blocks away, drive around the block to Sears to pick up vacuum bags, which brings me to the grocery store, my last stop. If something interferes with this plan, I will no doubt utter a few choice words to express my impatience. My tension and anxiety come from getting knocked out of my pre-planned orbit."

My physician friend says she has worked on changing her attitude about her type A traits. Nonetheless, she admits, "I still get impatient when people don't seem to have the same clarity of vision I have about something. I assume everybody gets it on the first presentation—you say it one time and that's enough. I used to think it was my job to see that people 'got it,' until my husband said, 'You are not the world's mother,' and a huge light bulb went on in my head."

Type A's are often the ones looking for a quicker way to do things. They depend on themselves and think they can handle the situation better than anyone else. They are direct and independent with a take-charge attitude. Take Dan, for example. He and his wife, Reba, set out down the Potomac River one evening in their small cabin cruiser. Finding a safe harbor, they anchored the boat on a protected inlet. At midnight they awoke to a fierce storm and a great banging and scraping of their hull against the river bottom.

"The boat had broken loose and we were in grave danger of running totally aground and overturning," explained Reba. "Dan tried starting the engine and throttling off the sand, but this did not work." Reba continued her story. "He called in a Mayday to the Coast Guard, but before they could arrive, Dan decided we would have to rescue ourselves. He went overboard into the tidal marsh and threw his body weight against the bow to point the boat off shore, with no success. I wasn't adept with the throttle, so we agreed to trade places. He gave me my life jacket and a flashlight, and I jumped into the water. I stood there throwing my body weight against the bow and we succeeded! But the wind and current were too strong for him to get back to me to get me on board."

Reba described the fear she felt as Dan left her to go for help from one of the boats anchored downstream. " 'I'll be right back,' he yelled as he pulled away, leaving me in the middle of this pitch-black swamp. Shortly he returned with someone and they pulled me up out of the sucking, black marsh bottom. As I was lifted into the boat, Dan called the Coast Guard to say we were both safe. Now that's what I call type A!"

Having some type A traits is not all bad. In fact, it can be healthy. It's all about *balance*. At its extreme, type A traits can lead to excessive competitiveness and self-destructive behaviors that put us in harm's way and alienate us from those who care for us. According to research by Dr. Redford Williams at Duke University, it is the hostility component in type A people that makes them more susceptible to coronary problems. A number of studies cite a relationship between high hostility scores and increased risk for various cardiovascular events.

If you want to work on changing unproductive type A behaviors, start by changing your attitude towards time, seeing it as a friend rather than an enemy. Work on slowing down, sitting still for a while. Accept that high levels of expressed anger and hostility constitute a problem. Focus on replacing anger and hostility with compassion and empathy. Learn to chill out!

Why is there so much interest in categorizing people? We are fascinated by labels and descriptions that make us feel that we accurately know ourselves or someone else. Some labeling of traits can help us to understand and accommodate to behaviors. But such labeling should not be used as evidence for judging ourselves or others. It is important to remember that each of us is wonderfully made, and that simple labels can never adequately capture our uniqueness.

12

First Things First

"IN THE EVENT OXYGEN IS REQUIRED, put on your own mask before assisting children or others," the flight attendant instructs passengers just before takeoff. The underlying meaning is clear: you will not be able to help those who depend upon you if you don't take care of yourself first. It's a lesson we have to learn over and over.

"If we women are so smart," a friend asked, "why do we get so confused about the difference between self-care and selfishness?"

Good question. Taking care of ourselves as women often is number eleven on our ten-item to-do list. But to be fair, when it comes to matters of health, men do not have a great record either. Often they eat foods that are less healthy, and they are less likely than women to go to a doctor. It's worth noting, though, that men are *more* likely than women to take a day off from work when they are sick.

Self-care is a central developmental task of women—and men—as we go through the steps of growth required of us as human beings. But there are aspects that are different for women. For example, our biological needs pose challenges men do not have to deal with. The whole reproductive process can make us feel vulnerable. Having another human being growing inside us can be daunting. It may be possible that, for these biological reasons, "taking care of ourselves" is more strongly related to age for women than for men.

Many women start taking better care of themselves after their children are grown. In my exercise class are a ninety-one-year-old woman, and another who originally joined in her seventies. Now somewhere in her eighties, she firmly claims, "Age is just a number, and mine is unlisted!"

Taking good care of ourselves is difficult for both sexes. As women, we should not put ourselves down for not doing more. Instead, we can celebrate that often we take better care of ourselves than do the men in our lives. We often outlive them and enjoy our golden years more because we are more likely to seek out doctors, mental health professionals, yoga and other meditative therapies, and group support.

Just as there is no one type of woman, there is no single strategy or approach to taking care of ourselves. Jean Johnson, a writer specializing in women's issues, offers a list of things women can do. Although her target audience is working moms, her suggestions apply to us all: get enough sleep; eat well; exercise; look your best; smile; count your blessings; ask for help; help others; connect to your spirituality, whether you find it in nature, in music, in art, in communal religion. We should also give ourselves permission to indulge in a little pampering from time to time. Get a massage; soak in the tub; find time to be alone; smell the roses; light our favorite candles; have a tea party for ourselves.

As women, we often "should" ourselves to death. Sometimes we are so wed to our role as caretaker that many of us become sick before we can say no to too many demands. As my friend surmised, we often do not see the difference between selfishness and self-nurturing. Women are much more likely than men to say that for them the worst thing about being sick is not that they feel bad or are in pain, but that they cannot take care of their family.

The good news is that there is a choice. We have the freedom to put our body on the list for regular care and maintenance. Each of us has the responsibility of taking loving care of our body, instead of pretending that *our* body will make an exception for us. The body will tell us what we need, if we are willing to slow down and pay attention. A wise person takes care of nagging little symptoms while they are still minor.

Obviously, taking care of ourselves does not mean just physically. Taking care of ourselves involves attending to emotional well-being—nurturing the spirit. Sometimes it's difficult to identify these needs and to know where to start. I suggest we start by doing something we've always wanted to do but haven't made time for. It's *never* too late to do something special for ourselves. Trust me, I know. I could be the poster child for the Late Bloomers Association. Recall that I took my first swimming lesson on my sixty-eighth birthday and soon was snorkeling off the coast of Cancun.

Recently, after turning seventy-two, I took the first dance lesson of my life. When I went into a studio to sign up, feeling somewhat embarrassed that I was probably the only woman in captivity who had never learned to dance, I made the defensive comment, "Now I'll *really* need to start at the beginning. I have two left feet."

The instructor smiled. "That's no problem. We usually begin by teaching people how to find their right foot." Reassured, I made an appointment for my first lesson, turned to leave, fell flat on my face, and skidded across the dance floor. Two other instructors raced over to help me up. My instructor said, "But in your case we'll make an exception and start by teaching you how to walk!"

Bruised but undaunted, I showed up three days later for my first-ever lesson. It was great fun! By the end of it the box step was my friend, and I signed up for more. It's amazing what a little mastery can do for self-esteem.

Some might say that fulfilling a long-standing desire to dance is silly or self-indulgent, but I believe that whatever puts a spring in our step and a smile on our face is right up there with oxygen. It's difficult to get too much of it. It is not selfish; it is self-care. In the long run, if we take responsibility for our own quality of life—our own dreams—we are less likely to become a burden to others. So, take care!

13

What's Up with Feeling Down?

"SINCE MY BROTHER WAS KILLED fourteen years ago," Edith said, "I have not allowed another family picture to be taken, even at holidays. It would be too painful to see a picture without him in it, because he was the life of the family." Edith's prolonged, unresolved grief reaction suggests she did not deal adequately and appropriately with her brother's death at the time. Now a depressive undercurrent runs through her existence that is insidious and draining, robbing her of the richness of her own life.

Loss and grief, if not processed and resolved, lead to depression. There are many other types of depression as well, including those that are associated with physical illnesses and chemical or hormonal imbalances. Did you know that about one in every five women and one in every ten men develop depression in their lifetime?

The good news is that no matter what form of depression a person suffers from, help is available. More than 80 percent of those who seek care for depression show improvement. The flip side is that without help and support, what disappears down the rabbit hole is the ability to live life fully.

Sometimes we do not know that the symptoms we're experiencing come from depression. "I was absolutely floored at age twenty-nine when my therapist suggested I might be depressed," my friend chuckled as she recounted the story long afterward. Her friends and loved ones certainly could see what was happening, and they struggled with whether or not to say anything.

After the death of her mother, my friend became short-tempered and irritable, finding fault with everything. She withdrew from extended family and friends and complained about activities she previously enjoyed. The thought that she might be depressed did not occur to her. After several months, as the situation worsened, her distraught husband finally said, "Honey, I love you, but I can't live with you this way. You have to do something."

My friend agreed to see a therapist, mainly to keep her husband from worrying. She was actually relieved when the therapist she consulted suggested she was depressed. "Me?" she said. "That never crossed my mind. I thought people around me were just getting on my nerves." Short-term counseling and an anti-depressant medication returned my friend to her energetic, happy, loving self.

We do not have to be professional diagnosticians to recognize common signs of depression in ourselves or in someone we love: prolonged sadness, tearfulness, or, as in my friend's case, irritability and withdrawal. We may suddenly exhibit uncharacteristic self-criticism, complain of disturbed sleep or low energy, or constantly express pessimism and harsh negativity toward people and formerly satisfying activities. If we do not want this painful state to continue, we can reach out and seek help.

Other signals may indicate that depression is lurking. "You're just no fun anymore" is a common observation depressed people hear from their friends and family. Depressed people are *not* fun to be around, and often they know that but don't know what to do about it.

"Why do I push people away at the time I need them most?" my depressed client asked. "I find myself getting upset with the stupidest little things, and I drive my friends right up the wall. Like last week, my cat had hairballs almost every day, and I cried each time my cat threw up! Let me tell you, it's hard to get any sympathy over a hairball," my depressed young friend said.

We need to be clear that seeking professional help, getting an accurate diagnosis, and following through on recommendations will help the one who is depressed *and* everyone around them. We may benefit from medication as well as counseling. We can ask a close friend or family member to make contacts and go with us for the first visit. Certainly we can avoid such unhelpful comments as, "I just need to get over this," or "I should just let it go and get on with life."

With help available, why is it that so many people suffering from depression do not reach out? What stops them from seeking help? In my years of clinical experience, I have seen denial in many forms: fear, pride, and ignorance lead people needing help to insist, "I can handle this on my own." They are afraid that seeking help means they're crazy. Many have said to me, "I don't believe in talking about your troubles, and I most certainly don't believe in taking medicine." Others say, "I must be weak not to be able to deal with this." Or, "I just need to be stronger. I need to pray more, to have more faith." Or even, "I must have done something wrong. Why is God punishing me?"

I assure them that depression is not punishment, not proof of sin, not due to a lack of faith. Depression is one response to being overwhelmed by physical or external circumstances. The body cannot absorb an infinite amount of hormonal activity, chemical change, or stress, or an infinite number of traumatic events. No one is to blame. It's the way we're made.

I believe that all the resources available to us are God-given, and that we are called upon to use these resources to live as full and rich a life as we can. For me, it's not an either-or situation. Do not look to medication as the magic bullet, but do not reject it without careful consideration. Don't give up your faith or spiritual outlook on life, and don't rule out professional help, either. Pray and meditate, if you choose, and also look at the role nutrition and exercise play in helping with depression.

Listen to your heart and intuition, but don't forget to engage your intellect to learn all about available medical and psychological resources. Sadness, pain, and loss are normal parts of living. Suffering is not optional. But remember, *there are no extra points for unnecessary suffering.* Over here is a life of love, laughter, and understanding. Over there is life of misery, complaints, and listlessness. Which way is up?

14

Run for Your Life!

"WITH MY HISTORY OF FIBROCYSTIC DISEASE, breast cancer had always been my greatest fear," my friend Kathy said. "When my gynecologist found a lump in my breast, the horror almost dropped me to my knees." A biopsy confirmed an estrogen-positive malignant tumor.

"They're both coming off," Kathy told her husband, Joe. "Recurrence is not that uncommon. I'm only doing breast cancer *one* time." With Joe's support, she underwent a bilateral mastectomy.

Determined to recover and to live a full life, Kathy resigned from her highly stressful job which for more than fifteen years had demanded too much of her time and energy. But giving up a successful career at an early age damaged her self-image and her sense of purpose. Grief and fear gripped her. Slowly Kathy began to see herself as a weak and helpless cancer patient, a lost soul who couldn't find meaning in her suffering. Changing this perception of herself was the focus of therapy.

After she celebrated the second anniversary of her surgery and was beginning a new job, Kathy, always a dedicated runner, decided to begin a year's training to run a marathon. Not long afterwards she also signed up for the Avon Walk for Breast Cancer. When the day of the event came, she had raised almost three thousand dollars from her friends and supporters for breast cancer research. Arriving at 6:15 a.m. at the "Wellness Village" with husband Joe by her side, Kathy was shocked to learn that participants would not be allowed to *run*. It was a walking marathon. The rules were explicit: "No MP3 players, no cell phones, NO RUNNING!" Kathy cringed. She had focused on running, knowing that others would walk. Somehow it had not registered with her that everyone would be restricted to the same activity. "Excuse me, did you say no running?" *What has my dream event turned into?*

The explanation involved something about liability. Reminding officials that she had signed a waiver did no good. Kathy began the event by walking like everyone else, and after a mile she began running. Joe checked on her periodically.

"Want a banana?" he asked.

"No, I want my iPod back!" She had counted on the music to keep her rocking and rolling through the miles. But there was no music player, there were no fans clapping, just shouted warnings from the van checking on the participants: "Stop running! Walk!" *Am I being shouted at for running? For being strong? For being determined?*

"Be careful—they'll stop you if they see you running," someone yelled as she approached the first rest stop. Kathy pointed to her "Survivor" cap and said, "Let them yell; I've been through a lot worse."

At each rest stop, the pressure mounted. "You are too far ahead," the organizers chided. "The Wellness Village isn't ready yet. We have been told to hold you for a while." Kathy realized that in order to finish the race she might have to leave the event.

"You know," she said to the volunteers, "this isn't about you; it's about me and about my supporters who believe in me." She stepped around the woman blocking her path and ran on.

Not having her music to rely on, she began every fifteen minutes to pray for a different family member she loved. Before she knew it, she had run more than fourteen miles. At mile 20, a staff member stepped directly in Kathy's path, scissors in hand, to cut Kathy's pink event bracelet off her wrist.

"You have to give your bracelet back, since you won't stop running." Kathy had removed the band from her wrist after the first confrontation. She handed it over and continued running. Now she was crying, feeling as though she wanted to scream.

Suddenly Joe came into view. "Want some company?" he asked. They ran together to the last rest stop, where his car was parked, and he drove ahead to meet her at the end. No cheering crowds, no banners, no hoopla. Just Joe standing there clapping. She had done it—26.2 miles—mostly running! Nothing would ever be the same for her.

"What was that like?" I asked.

"It was like complete success. I did it on my terms, and the person most important to me was there at the finish line. I learned that I am stronger than I had ever realized. I will never again be afraid to take a risk to achieve things important to me."

Kathy was radiant. "This race helped me know who I really am and how important my faith is. I have always been a play-by-the-rules person, but this time I was aware that I had obeyed higher rules. I had all these people who believed in me, and I wasn't going to let them down. I've never had that kind of high. I knew then that I *was* a survivor!"

Kathy's story reminds us that when the winds of suffering buffet us about, we can use those winds to fill our sails; that energy can be harnessed.

Then the suffering blows away old patterns and releases experiences of exhilaration and creative power. This transformation cannot be forced: it will happen over time. What may look like a monster is there to carry us to a new level of wonder and joy. I believe our job is not to fight, but to climb on the monster's back and ride it out. Like Kathy, we can survive because the monster we ride *is* survival, and the transformation which occurs in us is the new day dawning.

15

Think on These Things

"WHAT DOES BEAUTY MEAN TO YOU?" I asked more than two dozen people in my recent, very unscientific, poll. The responses went something like this: "Beauty is an inside thing." "Beauty is harmony." "Beauty is the inner makeup of a person, like the soul." "Beauty is natural—not manmade." "Beauty is an attitude, not a look." "Beauty is something of great value."

Many people I spoke with acknowledged that external beauty often resonates with our internal sense of joy and harmony. "When I was in college in Boone, North Carolina," Kevin said, "I thought Howard's Knob was absolutely beautiful in winter. There were no leaves, the mountain was stark—gray on gray. Later, I understood that my perception reflected the internal exhilaration and happiness I felt leaving home and beginning college."

Beauty has been described as whatever stimulates an immediate emotional response, accompanied by a feeling of pleasure. The stimulus may be "in the eyes," but could also be in the ear, the mouth, the nose, or the hands of the beholder. The emotional response is in the subjective experience of the beholder.

"I think beauty has been cheapened. It's now seen as a product for sale, which is sad," a friend said. Such a definition focuses on products and possessions that promise to bring glamour and beauty to our lives. For women, the promise is youth and physical attractiveness. For men, the promise is primarily sexual.

In contrast, my friend's view is that beauty is an inner strength and peace of mind. "My inner serenity is directly proportional to the harmony and order I experience in nature," she says. "If I get too busy and preoccupied to enjoy the birds or cloud formations or the stars, I begin to feel sick mentally and spiritually."

Nature offers us the balanced perfection and rhythm of watching the seasons, the cycles of the tides, the flow of generations. Experiencing a sense of eternity is to experience profound beauty. What is required is a certain attention, whether maintaining a beautiful garden or creating a harmonious space in one's home. "My need to experience beauty," one person said, "is a cry from within me to compensate for the cruelty and brutality and the suffering in the world."

Some people treat the perception of beauty as a judgment. This is appropriate for teens who are busy sorting out their peers. It's one of the gifts of the aging process that we grow beyond such frantic judgments. I think of beauty as subjective, changing with the growth of the individual. Kahlil Gibran, the writer of *The Prophet*, offered a definition of beauty as "eternity gazing at itself in a mirror." Indian poet and novelist Rabindranath Tagore described beauty as "truth's smile."

While our culture seems to focus on external trappings that it defines as beautiful, we can think of beauty not as either/or, but as *both* internal and external. When we are in harmony with ourselves and with life, we can go inside and find beauty. But our spirit requires matter in order to manifest itself. What would life be like if the force of beauty could not be manifest in the color and fragrance of flowers, or in the simple smile of a child?

When external ugliness is beyond our control, however, inner beauty can suffice. We can have frightful external appearances and still be beautiful on the inside—witness the highly successful television show *Ugly Betty,* whose title character is intelligent and altruistic. Her caring shines through her unfashionable outward appearance. But no amount of external beauty can compensate for internal ugliness.

A woman I know shared with me a childhood experience that forever changed her views about beauty. When she was seven years old, she was hit in the face with a tomato stake hurled by her young friend as they were playing. She fell to the ground, hands warm and sticky with blood. She could see concern on her mother's face as she cradled her up in her arms and sped to the hospital. Blood gushed from the place where part of her cheek was now missing.

"What's going to happen to me?" she asked.

"They're going to put some stitches in your face," her mother said.

"Is it going to hurt?"

"I think the doctor will put you to sleep, so you won't feel anything." Later, as the little girl lay in the hospital bed, she mouthed to her mother, through heavy bandages covering her face like a cast, "Am I going to be ugly?"

Her mother held her hand. "Don't worry," she said. "I have been praying all the time they were stitching you up. I have put you in God's hands, and He has told me you will be beautiful on the inside."

"I believed my mother," she told me. "And that has made all the difference."

It is easy to see inner beauty, but it is hard sometimes to remember to look. Any effort spent in creating harmony and beauty is going in the right direction.

Walter Russell, whose words never fail to resonate deeply with me, suggests that our role in developing inner beauty as his life's philosophy: "I will see beauty and goodness in all things. From all that is unlovely shall my vision be immune."

lesson three

The Knack of Being Happy with Parents and Siblings

Something has happened
To my understanding of existence
That now makes my heart always full of wonder
And kindness.

—HAFIZ

An influential teacher I know tells her students that no one can become a competent professional until he or she can take pride in their origins, to accept their personal history, and find things to love and cherish in their deepest roots. The good news is that it is never too late to have a happy childhood, to parent ourselves, to change our myopic view of our early years, replacing it with the perspective of an adult—to stop blaming and start living.

16

Memories Are Made of This

ONE OF THE MOST SUCCESSFUL AND INFLUENTIAL teachers I've known told her students that no one can become a competent professional until he can take pride in his origins. The professor's goal was to teach students to accept their personal history and find things to love and cherish in their deepest roots. "Until you learn that, you are incomplete," she told her college students over and over. My teacher friend spoke with authority. Her words came from a deep well of struggle and suffering. As a child of alcoholics, she had ranted and raved, demeaned and denied her heritage for many, many years.

My friend Dorothy provided me with a powerful image when she described her childhood as a pizza. "When I was younger," she said, "the slice that was my parents' alcoholic behavior was the only piece I saw. Now if I can step back and see the whole pizza—if I am not focused on one sick slice—I no longer have to work hard to accept and love my family." It was not until she came to understand and accept her parents as whole but flawed people suffering from a killer illness that she herself became fully whole and integrated.

It is a great tribute to my family of origin that I find no shame in being the eighth out of nine children born to sharecropper parents during the Great Depression. I sing along with Loretta Lynn when she belts out, "I'm proud to be a coal miner's daughter." My parents never made it beyond elementary school, but they understood life and encouraged me to embrace it. I learned from my mother what unconditional love means. I learned early what it takes to be a good parent. Is it financial security? No. Freedom from disease? No. Social status? No. All of these can be helpful, but they are not the essential ingredients.

Learning to cope with our family of origin requires that we come to see them as whole persons—just like ourselves. Being happy with family is a decision we have to make, and it requires perspective. We have all been parented by someone. And for good or ill, our first impressions and experiences are the longest lasting. Why is this? Because as young children we are malleable and vulnerable. We can't make sense of things. We don't understand about illnesses, stress, financial concerns. We may feel unsafe and unprotected.

Even if our early years weren't perfect, it is never too late to reinterpret childhood in order to focus on the whole pizza, to stop blaming the past and start living in the present. Blame is a game we *choose* to play, and we can opt out of that game any time we're ready. It's always a good idea to ask ourselves this question: If I'm not happy with what I'm doing, then who am I trying to please? My mother or father? My sister? My child?

One of my clients spent his entire life in the shadow of his older, highly successful brother. As a young boy he made choices about his friends, his activities, even what high school courses he would sign up for, based on what his older brother had chosen. He tried to emulate his sibling but could never do what he had done, no matter how hard he tried. In time he became angry at him and envied his successes. He developed elaborate explanations as to why his brother was more successful than he. His perceptions of early childhood experiences in which his brother had been favored over him occupied his thoughts.

But some of the things he "remembered" from those years never happened. Being trapped in the shadow of his brother had become his life story. It was his choice. As far as I could tell, this was not something his sibling had encouraged. Certainly his brother wasn't going to get him out of it.

It takes work to get out of such a rut. The knack of a happy life is always being sure I'm living my own life to the fullest—growing up out of my roots toward the sunshine.

17

Family Reunions

My sister Gloria, the family organizer, makes her home available for family reunions that always include a feast of Southern delicacies. Along with baked ham, roast turkey, and two pans of dressing, the table groans with butter beans, squash, corn, green beans, turnips, sliced tomatoes, watermelon, potato salad, and corn bread. Stories flow as everyone drinks sweet iced tea and refills their plates, telling themselves aloud that they must save room for at least one of the several homemade desserts.

I have often made it clear to everyone that I love to hear stories of our shared past, otherwise known as family history. Each sibling has a story to tell, and the house fills with laughter and arguments over whether the story being told is entirely accurate. Whether greeted with "I remember that," or "Now, that's not the way I heard it," the storyteller insists that his or her version is the gospel truth.

At these reunions, I have learned things about my older siblings, now deceased, that I had not known. On one recent occasion it was big news to me to discover that, with only a fourth-grade education, my oldest brother, Frank, was elected coroner in the small town of Roberta many years ago.

"He made twenty-five dollars each time he was called to declare somebody dead," my brother Walt told us.

"What happened if the cause of death was uncertain?" I wanted to know.

Walt laughed. "As I recall, Frank never was called to a death that he found suspicious. Breathing or not breathing seemed to be the only decision to be made." Frank's elementary rule of thumb made him popular with the town officials who could save time and money not having to bother with autopsies.

Not only was the my-brother-the-coroner story news to me, I did not know that my pacifist sister Ruth had been a sharpshooter and had once shot a snake in a hen's nest without hurting the hen or breaking any eggs. "She absolutely did it," my brother Walt said. "But if she ever shot a gun again, I didn't know it."

Each one at the table takes a turn sharing some special memory, and the hours pass quickly. "Do you remember . . . ," someone asks, and the answer is yes if the person is being presented in a good light, no if the story makes us look bad. We all have selective recall, and we are sure that our personal recollection is the truth of the event.

Family reunions, at their best, help us mend connections worn thin by distance and the passage of time. They allow us opportunities to be vulnerable, to share long-cherished feelings or air old hurts and misunderstandings. They provide the opportunity to reframe our thoughts and expectations. They remind us of the importance of belonging, and of our shared faith in the imperfect institution of family. Accepting family flaws allows us to hold on to what is important and not get mired in aspects of relationships that are unhealthy.

As the day ends and we say our good-byes, I realize that it is not the content of what has been said these past few hours, but the process of saying it, that is important. It does not matter that some stories have more of a ring of truth than others. What matters is that the family can still, after all these years, look forward to coming together and sharing memories. We are still connected, still caring, still supportive, still forgiving. Today we all had a chance to share our favorite stories, and to draw strength from the sharing.

Reunion suggests connectedness or returning to a state of unity: to re-unite, remind, recollect, reframe. As I share stories from my own family reunions, I am painfully aware that for many, family reunions look nothing like the ones I am blessed to be a part of.

For some, just the thought of a family reunion instills fear and anxiety. For many who were abused or neglected as children, for adult children of alcoholics, and many others, a happy family reunion is the last thing they can imagine. Yet they may go to family gatherings out of a sense of obligation or guilt: if you are good, we tell ourselves, you honor traditions. Or we go with high expectations that *this* time it will be wonderful.

It is a shared myth that family traditions deserve to be honored and continued. We need to make our own careful assessment about what is healthy and life-giving, and what is destructive. We need to be aware that we are creating the stories the next generation will tell.

Like many traditions, family reunions can be magical, adding sparkle to our lives, but they can also be stressful and anxiety-provoking. Family reunions can lead to overwhelming expectations, disappointments, and exhaustion. Unless we pace ourselves, reduce our expectations, and set limits for ourselves, our serenity and sense of genuine connectedness can be lost in turmoil.

Family reunions aren't an automatic cure for all our past relationship problems. In dealing with these stresses, it helps if we don't tune in to all the high expectations and instead stay tuned to our inner self—to who we are.

And we need to know that we can substitute new traditions for old ones.

Tradition is defined as customs or practices long observed. If the traditions we are invited to participate in fail to nurture our spirit, we can choose to start our own traditions—for ourselves, our families, friends, loved ones. Creating new traditions that bring healing and growth *is* possible.

I have a friend who chose to live five hundred miles and three states away from her family, who seemed in constant turmoil. For a long time, whenever she returned home, she got caught up in arguments and tensions and left upset. She did not get a kick out of one-upping her siblings, or arguing with her father about her career choice. The supercharged atmosphere that seemed to fuel her family members was painful to her. So she started a new tradition. Now when she returns for a visit, as she approaches the street where she grew up she visualizes a sign above her parents' home that reads, DANGER ZONE. She imagines herself in a protective robe, safe and secure. Holding onto this image, she can enjoy her visit, make small talk, express interest in her family, and not get trapped in painful conflicts.

There is no end to the healthy new customs people create. My friend Jean shared one she participates in with her family that I find particularly appealing. Each New Year's Eve her family gathers around the dining table. A brown ceramic box is in the center. Each persons writes down a wish for the coming year—something they long for that would make them really happy. Each wish is placed in the box, which then sits on the living room mantel until the following New Year's Eve, when each family members reads aloud what had been wished for on the previous occasion and talks about the outcome. Then the process is repeated. This sharing with one another has become so important that family members rarely miss this event.

It is never too late to create strong, healthy bonds that affirm what is best in family relationships. As the years pass, these new traditions will comfort and nurture us, helping us to live grace-filled lives.

18

Be It Ever So Humble

"WE'RE HAVING 'A LITTLE BROWN JUG FESTIVAL and Blast from the Past' in late May and we want you to come." The invitation was from one of the festival committee members and I was both surprised and intrigued. I wanted to know more about this celebration being planned for my little hometown of Roberta, Georgia.

The letter went on. "The Historical Society will also be holding a Fund Raiser Chicken-Q to fund a new roof for the county courthouse. We would like to have you come and participate, since you are one of our treasures." A treasure—oh my! I was honored. My hometown had called me back from time to time to celebrate my origins. This time, the organizers and I exchanged several e-mails, and I learned that as part of the celebration, a speaker would present the life of the Indian agent Benjamin Hawkins, buried near Roberta, whose monument was the centerpiece of this one-traffic-light town when I was growing up there.

The invitation set me thinking about Colonel Hawkins and specifically about the role the monument dedicated to him had played in my life as a young girl raised within its shadow. I did not know it at the time, but, according to the commemorative booklet prepared by the Crawford County

Sesquicentennial Celebration, I grew up in a county rich in history. And my hometown of Roberta was the heart of these historic activities. Such glory was hard for me to believe. The booklet proclaimed that "the greatest civic event ever occurring in Roberta was the unveiling of the Monument to Benjamin Hawkins, who died in 1816." The unveiling of a memorial in Roberta erected by the United States government, and I missed it! The monument arrived two years before I made my entrance into the world.

As a kid in Roberta I passed the tall, gray stone monolith with identical black plaques on all four sides several times a day. One of the many houses we lived in looked out on this centerpiece of town. The plaza surrounding it was the place where farmers parked their wagons to shop for feed and grain. And occasionally members of the Garden Club would stop to pull up a few weeds or to plant seed for zinnias to grow, though the seed never seemed to break through the soil and provide the beauty the club hoped for.

When I was a teenager, the monument served as a backdrop for Virgil Vinson's three-hour sermons, delivered each Saturday afternoon. Beginning around two p.m., Virgil, a local farmer and a self-ordained preacher, arrived in his one-horse wagon, tied his mule to a shade tree nearby, and walked briskly to the monument, Bible in hand.

Virgil paced back and forth, waving his Bible in the air or pounding it on his palm to punctuate his preaching. Within an hour his white shirt, sleeves rolled above his elbows, and his khaki pants would be soaked with perspiration. Huge drops of sweat dripped from his face. His wiry gray hair stood on end. He preached about hellfire and damnation, about repentance and forgiveness, about how those who were not saved would experience God's wrath.

Virgil's raspy voice could be heard all over town, though by the second hour of shouting he began to sound hoarse and the rhythm changed to a slower pace. By then Virgil would begin to use his sleeve to dab the froth around his mouth and to catch the beads of sweat dropping from his bushy eyebrows. He preached until he collapsed in exhaustion, then he'd recover and untie his mule, climb on the wagon, and quietly ride out of town.

Folks never gathered around Virgil to hear him preach, and no one ever went up to speak to him afterwards. I wondered if he was aware that he didn't have an attentive congregation—or if it would have mattered, had he known.

The sesquicentennial commemorative booklet expanded my understanding of the importance of the Hawkins Monument beyond its service as an anchor point for Virgil. How could I have been so myopic?

Colonel Benjamin Hawkins, the first white man to settle in Crawford County, was "a man of letters, a mediator of peace, faithful unto death. . . . After the beginning of the Revolutionary War, he became a member of General George Washington's staff. . . . Later he went to Georgia to assume jurisdiction over all the Indian Tribes south of the Ohio River. He kept the peace between the Indians and white settlers for many years."

The sesquicentennial booklet provided additional information about Colonel Hawkins. The part of the booklet that got my attention was this: "The Creek women were respected by Hawkins and he began having them instructed in spinning and agriculture. The males resented this somewhat. They feared the females would become too independent."

Reading that statement, I felt disappointed that I had not been on hand for "the greatest civic event ever occurring in Roberta." I knew that I would have liked Benjamin Hawkins.

Colonel Hawkins is buried outside Roberta. I asked recently about directions to his grave site. Here's what I learned. Get to Roberta any way you can. Then, "take GA 128 south from Roberta to Hortman's Store. It will be the first paved street to the left. Go about .4 miles. This road is a dead end road. There is only one grave in the cemetery. Hawkins, Benjamin, Col. 1754–1816—U.S. Senator, Creek Indian Agent."

Sadly for me, I was not able to attend the Little Brown Jug Festival. Being invited back as "one of our treasures," fifty years after I left this tiny town of then 600 people—most of whom knew me and rooted for me to make it when I left—reminded me that though the roads I have traveled during the past half century have taken me to faraway places, I am still connected to this little dot on the map. The Hawkins monument, still standing tall and proud in the center of town, serves as an anchor not only for the community, but as an important reminder of my roots and heritage as well.

19

Sisterhood

"LORD HELP THE MISTER WHO COMES BETWEEN me and my sister," Irving Berlin wrote in his song "Sisters." These words speak to the strength of our relationships with our sisters. Then, true to life, the line that follows twists in a different direction: "And Lord help the sister who comes between me and my man."

Sisters, like flowers in a garden, come in all shapes and sizes. Sometimes our personalities and temperaments are so different that it is difficult to believe that we came from the same parents. Older sister Leslie wore overalls, boots, no makeup, and long hair. Her fashionable younger sister, Sherrie, was thin and always carefully dressed, wearing the perfect shade of lipstick. One year, Leslie sent her younger sister a birthday card with the following message inscribed: "On your birthday, I love you so much I will do anything for you—including helping you look for your real parents."

The sisters our parents present to us are the luck of the draw. They can become our best friends, or we can be yoked together unhappily at a very young age. I believe that these early family dynamics with our sisters color our feelings about ourselves and our relationships with other women. I know that the relationship I had with my oldest sister, Ruth, colors *every* relationship I have now.

With nine children, my parents were stretched to the limit and beyond. They were scratching a living out of the dirt during the 1930s when I was born. I had seven older siblings. Thirteen months after my birth, another baby came along, and Ruth, seventeen at the time, took over my care. We had a special bond not shared by our other siblings. She died of cancer when she was twenty-nine and I was twelve. I was with her when she died, and her last words to me provided a framework for what I would become and how I would view my role in life, including some of the worst decisions I ever made. In the last hours before her death she held my hand and told me how much she loved me, and how she knew I would use all my talents.

"It isn't how long you live that matters," she whispered as she squeezed my hand. "What matters is how much you care. Promise me that you will always care about people." I promised. Keeping that promise has been both a blessing and a burden. The impact on my twelve-year-old psyche was such that I have had to struggle for a self-image that can embrace and cope with the cobras of the world.

Family-of-origin dynamics are always with us. If things are not going well in the present, it can help if we look for places in which we are bound by the past. It's worth sitting down and evaluating the impact of having—or not having—a sister; of having or not having brothers. It helps to be aware of birth order, of growing up in a single-parent home, of the lasting effects of intense rivalry between siblings.

Recently I overreacted when a casual acquaintance put pressure on me to give him more time and attention with a medical problem than I was willing to give. Seeing my distress, a friend suggested that my reaction might have its roots in my relationship to my younger sister, who suffered from severe asthma as a child. She was right. Growing up, I believed I somehow was responsible for keeping her from getting upset, persuading her to take her medicine, and driving her to the hospital when she could barely breathe and her nails turned blue from lack of oxygen. The weight of responsibility felt terrifying to me.

I share this story because none of us is immune to such experiences. It is important to seek conscious awareness so that we then have choices about how we will react. Raising to consciousness the root of my overreaction allowed me to accept my feelings. I was then free to offer the support and care that I *was* willing to give to the person asking for my help.

Sometimes journaling or painting can help us get in touch with feelings we are not aware of. My friend sketched a picture of her brother in full military dress uniform, with epaulets on his broad shoulders. She wasn't sure what this drawing meant.

"Oh," her therapist said when she saw it, "he's the anointed one in your family."

My friend found it helpful to make conscious what she had on some deep level known all her life, that in her family, her brother was indeed the favored one. Being aware of that, she could choose how she would react. She could clean up some old issues and begin to enjoy her brother.

Thinking about siblings and the meaning of those relationships reminds us that each of us plays a role in our family drama. It helps to know what our role in the family has been so we can decide if we want to accept it, or if we want to try out for another part more suited to us. We may find it possible to choose the role of loving, supportive friend and family member, despite grudges or bad blood from the past.

Those who do not have biological siblings often seek out friends who become soul mates. In any case, we have the opportunity to *become* the sister or brother we always wanted to have in our lives.

20

Taking Care of Aging Parents

FOR MANY OF US, THE TIME WILL COME when we will be called on to take care of our aging parents. We know it can happen, but we may not be prepared for when or how, or the consequences of this change.

Aging parents often need a variety of things, some of which we can give them and some we can't. We have to be clear with ourselves and with them about the limits of our time, finances, and emotions.

The wisdom for dealing with our parents in this new way is not always at our fingertips. When we are children, our parents are everything. We look to them for validation, advice, and support. They are our anchors. As our parents begin to "fail"—to have problems that affect their bodies and their minds—we have to realize that instead of looking to our parents to give us support and protection, the tide turns and we may resent their needing these very things from us.

A close friend was dealing with the impending death of her father. Although she is a highly regarded physician, her father, living the final months of his life in her home, had never seen her as an accomplished woman. One big issue for adult children in situations like this, she said, is that even when parents give you permission for decision making, they often do not show respect for your abilities to make the best decisions.

She's right. We are forced to make decisions that parents don't want. Why should they show respect? It feels like a setup. Negative feelings are guaranteed in this situation. We are given incredible responsibilities, often with no tangible appreciation or recognition.

My friend wrote to me about how she coped with this: "Assuming a caretaker role with my father has gradually awakened in me forgiveness of the weakness of the man that my father was. I have come to realize that his illness no longer enables him to march about as fearless and brutish. In almost an instant my heart has turned to jelly regarding all of his past indignities, insults, and assaults. He is recycling to the frail, lonely child he must have once been, and I can only open my arms and heart further to take him in. He seemed shy as he watched me all day deal with the movers, reset all the electronics, and put together a small haven for him downstairs that incorporates safety, art, function, and love. For the first time ever, I think my father sees me as competent, and he is ever so grateful. I sense it, and so my anger has dissipated like fog under the sun."

One of the most important lessons we need to learn in taking care of our parents is how to honor them even when they cannot honor us. In order to have the peace and wisdom to honor our parents, we must also honor ourselves. Paramount in this process is taking care of our own needs. We must pay attention to our health; get enough sleep; exercise; plug in some fun; take a break when we feel the pressure building; talk with someone about our feelings and needs. Support can be found from friends, clergy, a professional counselor. We need a community of support because alone we simply cannot do the job with grace. Sometimes our caregiving must go on for years, often with increasing demands and needs for higher levels of care until death finally comes. Within a community of support we can find the wisdom and grace to do the job well.

I was in my late forties and living in Boston when my mother had a serious fall and had to be taken to a nursing home in the small Georgia town where she lived. I still recall the anguish and guilt I felt that I was so far away and unable to leave my job and family and go help take care of her. My sister had her own guilt. She had promised Mama that she would never send her to a nursing home, but now she was forced to accept this as the best solution. In situations like this, guilt is one of the most common visitors to our hearts and minds, and if we're not careful, it can take up permanent residence there.

Another problem in caring for our parents is a shift in the balance of power. Having power should not mean that we abuse it, that we hold it over our parents. It means having the power to forgive, to let go of resentments, and to extend the compassion it takes to heal suffering. It is the living example of good over evil and the power of bringing light to a dark situation. Having power in such a situation allows us to choose transformation through compassion, rather than running roughshod over our parents' feelings.

Nurturing our parents through this dark and murky period is difficult and requires much of us. Our goal should be to become for our parents the kind of person that either they were for us or that we wish they had been. We all will someday have the opportunity of dying. Contemplating that reality helps make us compassionate towards our aging parents. Honoring our parents the way we would want to be honored as we age is the Golden Rule in action.

This essay was originally titled "Parenting Our Parents." But the truth is that we *cannot* parent our parents. They cannot become our children, nor should we want them to. If taking care of our aging parents is not called parenting, then what is it called? I believe it's called nurturing, caring, commitment, dedication, sacrifice, pain, frustration, satisfaction, transformation, joy. In the final analysis, it is called love.

21

Dinnertime

"My parents don't want me in their home or in their lives," said Cassie, a sullen, depressed, suicidal adolescent as she sat in my Boston office many years ago.

There was no particular emotion associated with this startling statement. I wondered what it was about her parents' behavior that could be so convincing that this teenager had twice tried to take her life. I accepted her invitation to visit her home, an expensive condominium in a prestigious high-rise building overlooking the Charles River.

It was a bitter cold, blustery winter day when I arrived. Cassie met me at the door. Her parents weren't home, though they knew I was stopping by. The condo had one bedroom for the parents, and an alcove with a cot for their daughter. There were pictures of her parents and friends throughout the house, but no pictures of Cassie. Most startling to me was the kitchen. The small breakfast nook held a tiny table with two chairs, two placemats, two sets of silverware, two coffee mugs. It was then that I got it. There *was* no room for her in her parents' lives—especially at the dining table.

I never forgot that scene. But the story has a happy ending. In therapy, Cassie found that her worth did not depend on her parents' view of her, and that she was a valued person. She began to participate in school athletics, volunteered as a peer counselor in a pilot program, and was invited to live with her aunt and uncle, who paid for her to attend a local community college.

A few years later I participated in the design and implementation of a research project to identify factors for adolescents that protected them against risk of self-destructive behavior. I worked with researchers from Boston University and Simmons College School of Social Work to develop questionnaires and open-ended interview protocols. Almost as an aside, we added a question for the adolescent interview: "How often each week does your family sit down at the dinner table for a meal together?"

The responses to this question proved to be more important than we could have imagined. When the study was complete and all the data had been analyzed, one of the strongest protectors against risk of self-destructive behavior turned out to be eating at least one family meal together each week! To me, this was amazing. Having a family meal at least once a week could be that significant? Yes, adolescents seemed to be saying.

Years later, research continues to bear witness to the impact that this remarkably simple activity has on young people. Public service announcements now encourage families to share meals together as a way of reducing risky behavior in children and adolescents. A study reported in the August 2005 issue of the *Archives of Pediatrics and Adolescent Medicine* shows that family meals can enhance the health and well-being of teens and adolescents. Researchers found that the more often families ate together, the less likely teens were to use cigarettes, alcohol, or marijuana. In addition, a higher frequency of family meals was associated with fewer depressive symptoms, higher grade-point averages, and fewer suicide attempts among middle school and high school students.

The research suggests that the lasting effects of the family dinner table, or lack of it, persists regardless of parents' marital, social, or economic status. Interestingly, the overall effects, while significant for boys, appeared stronger for girls. Ideally, the family meal encourages healthy balanced eating, conversation, and the resulting development of parent mentoring and relationship building.

Making sense of who you are as an adult is enhanced by something as simple as taking the time to reflect on what mealtimes were like for you growing up. A fruitful exercise is to take a sheet of paper and draw a sketch of your family's dinner table. Who was there? Where did each family member usually sit? Why? What do you notice as you draw? If negative memories arise, let them. In that case, you might ask yourself what your dinner table looks like now. How might you change it to be a positive experience for you?

My own family dinner table was a rough, handmade wooden table, with a long wooden bench on one side for my siblings and me. My father sat at one end of the table, my uncle who lived with us sat at the other end, and my mother sat on the side nearest the wood stove. All three sat in unfinished cane-bottom chairs. A kerosene lamp in the center of the table burned brightly at night, illuminating the red checkered oilcloth covering the table. My mother did all the cooking, having the evening meal on the table when my father, uncle, and older siblings came in from the farm. I remember very little conversation at the table. My parents were tired after a hard day's work. All our food was raised on the farm, and meals were predictable and utilitarian. But I remember the sense of connectedness I felt eating with family, often in silence. I knew how hard my mother worked cooking everything "from scratch" on a wood stove, with no refrigerator and no appliances.

Looking back, I see that this early childhood experience has had a major influence on my attitudes about food and preparing meals today. I am not particularly interested in food, except to eat well for health reasons. I do not enjoy cooking, although I can prepare good meals. Preparation of fancy meals seems like a lot of work to me, and I avoid it whenever possible. I love dinnertime meals with family and friends, whether eating in or at a restaurant, but I have little interest in which restaurant we go to, or what's being served. I enjoy the ambience, the experience of being together, of sharing. My family and friends know this about me, and offer good-natured teasing. "Look," I tell them, "I love you so much I don't risk your lives by cooking for you!"

lesson four

The Knack of Being Happy with Friends and Community

Out
Of a great need
We are all holding hands
And climbing.
Not loving is a letting go.

—HAFIZ

Friends and community are important to us because we need a context within which we say, "I exist; I'm here." When we leave home we move into an ever-expanding world. Imagine, as a child, standing in front of a globe as big as your house. If you are rooted in front of South America, you naturally assume that the world consists only of South America. As we venture out and see new things, our perceptions change. What are we to make of it all?

There are many possible responses to this universal experience: disillusionment; fear of the unfamiliar; curiosity to know more. There is the tension of wanting to retreat to safety and wanting the thrill of moving into a new adventure. Another term for this tension is stress. Our community and our friends can help us feel connected instead of fearful and overwhelmed.

"Tell me what independence means," I asked a seven-year-old boy whose parents were farmers. He didn't hesitate. "Well, it's like when you're a baby calf and you want to stand up on your four wobbly legs and you don't want no help." It takes time to learn what we can do on our own and when we need to ask for help.

Accepting life on its own terms is a lifelong process. Along the way it is very important who we choose as friends. There's an old saying that if you lie down with dogs, you get up with fleas, which is a colorful way of explaining how we are influenced by the habits and attitudes of the people around us. If you want a happy life, seek out happy people. Find groups where positive values are honored.

Happiness in community comes from an understanding of why we bond: for safety, learning, transition from family, celebration, mutual aid, comfort, fun. In the biblical book of Genesis we read, "It is not good for the man to be alone." Regardless of one's theology, from a psychological point of view, this statement has great import. The need to belong ranks right after our need for food and shelter. Healthy adjustment includes connection to the world and feeling part of the human race. I need to know that I am a valuable part of my community, as valuable as every other person, and that what makes me strong and happy naturally benefits others. The hallmark of depression is withdrawal and isolation from others.

We spend relatively little time in our family of origin, and most of our lifespan elsewhere—working out the issues formed in and by our early experiences. It is never too late to create a healthy community for yourself. Don't let community just happen to you. Know who you are and find a community that is compatible. If you know who you are; if the community you're in doesn't make you happy; if it brings dread and fear—move on. Decide what you want. Don't wait; reach out for it.

We need to create a community that allows the heart to sing. Life is hard—at best. Connections give us the courage to go forward, through fear, tension, and stress. We are all in this together. As we grow older, community and friends advance in importance, while family decreases in importance.

As my older friend is fond of saying, "Well, every tub has to set on its own bottom, but without friends and community, you fare tough." Who wants old age to extend another twenty or thirty years if they are miserable years? I like belonging to a group that holds me to account. It doesn't mean that I always get my way, but within its framework I can both give and take comfort. I work on projects that are worthwhile to me and are a great source of happiness. It doesn't matter what the project is, if it does no one harm, if it catches my imagination and gives me energy.

22

Under the Covers

MUCH OF WHAT I NEEDED TO KNOW about friends I learned sitting beneath a series of colorful handmade quilts that my mother, my older sister, and our neighbors gathered around twice each week to work on. I was allowed to play quietly or read silently underneath the frames holding the quilting materials in place.

It was under the quilts that I learned how to read. I missed out on first and second grades as I recovered from a series of illnesses, including diphtheria and hepatitis, and I waited each day for my older siblings to return from school so I could read their books. There were no newspapers or magazines in our rambling old farmhouse, so I eagerly read everything their teachers assigned to my teenaged brother and sister.

The women from neighboring farms who came to quilt viewed the occasion as a social one, and they always seemed eager to catch up on the local gossip. Their skillful hands would settle the quilting frames into place, quickly attach the backing, and roll out a layer of cotton batting. The women took turns providing a patchwork top painstakingly made at home and brought to our living room to be quilted.

Each week I claimed my central position underneath the frames, sitting cross-legged, reading or writing as the quilting activity began and continued throughout the afternoon. After a while I'd have trouble concentrating on anything except the wonderful stories being shared by these mostly faceless women who each week took their same seats around the quilting circle, where they shared with each other their most intimate thoughts. I enjoyed a warm feeling of being a silent witness to the strength of these women, who were so open and honest and trusting.

Although I was too young to participate in their work, I loved the intimacy of my special vantage point where I could watch their needles rhythmically pierce in and out of the backing fastened to the worn wooden frames.

Quilting was serious business, with a quilt completed every two weeks and taken home by one of the quilters to be used to warm the cold winter nights. Each woman took home one quilt every three months—four new quilts every year for each household. It was my first experience with the concept of community, and I slowly became aware of how powerful this experience was.

Patterns for quilting were selected from pictures in catalogs, which someone brought. Sea Shells, Grandmother's Fan, Flower Garden, Log Cabin. And I was happy when occasionally I was allowed to pick the pattern for the quilt about to be started, or to pass out the thimbles kept safely in a cardboard matchbox on our mantel.

I knew each of the women well from the knees down. The minister's wife, Nellie, always sat next to Mama, her stockings rolled into tight little knots just below her knees. Varicose veins ran like spider webs down to her black Dr. Scholl's. Each week she began by sharing church news and updating the prayer list. Mama, who always quilted barefoot, sat next to Nellie and could be counted on for a humorous comment when the conversation became tense. "Mary Julia, I swear, you can find the light side to any calamity," Nellie would say. "God must have put you here to lighten up our hearts."

Our nearest neighbor, Ella Mae, walked the two miles of dusty road each week to join them. She wasted no time getting seated next to Mama, often heaving a sigh of relief as she pulled her homemade feed-sack sundress up around her thighs and extended her legs so that her high-top tennis shoes brushed against me. It was Ella Mae who punctuated the air frequently with outbursts of "Praise the Lord" or "Hallelujah!"

Carlene took lead chair on the other side of the quilt, a fitting position for the most strong-willed, outspoken, and courageous of the group. Her feet always arrived under the quilt with well-trimmed red toenails and the first ankle bracelet I had ever seen. Carlene covered a wide range of topics each week and held her listeners spellbound as she recounted tales of other women in the county—"sisters," she called them. She accepted everyone, passed no judgment, and seemed devoid of doubt or dismay no matter what news she had to report. She was interested in strong women, and she made it plain to those listening to her each week that we should all admire and support women "with a mind of their own, and not afeared to use it."

Mama always shifted her callused feet and wiggled her stubby toes whenever Carlene used the word "pregnant." It was a word she considered far too intimate—too abrupt—to be spoken aloud. (Mama felt the same way about the word "dead." To hear her tell it, no one ever died, they just "passed on" or "crossed over.") And as for "pregnant," Mama preferred instead to announce that a woman was "gone again" or was "in the family way." She herself had been in that condition nine times; most of us had been born in this very house where now her friends shared their experiences with life and death.

My oldest sister, Ruth, sat opposite Mama and seemed to have a strong need to keep both the conversation and the quilting on track. She was the only quilter who preferred to work in cotton slacks and white socks, no matter what the temperature. I wondered as I occasionally leaned my head against her knees if the others knew that her slacks hid terrible scars, the result of her having crawled into an open fire as a curious eighteen-month-old. The blonde wig and the scar on her left cheek surely were obvious remnants of that disaster, but soft cotton clothes could hide some of the old hurts.

Next to Ruth sat Hattie, whose bare legs and feet bore small scrapes and bruises that changed each week. Hattie's toes were permanently crossed over each other as if she were making wishes with her feet while her slender fingers deftly put her needle through its paces.

Each week it seemed that someone had experienced hard times, and they were unabashedly grateful to their fellow quilters for the help they received. When a tearful Hattie shared the news that her barn, filled with food for the winter, had been struck by lightning and burned, she left the quilting session with meat from our smokehouse, potatoes from our potato hills, and the promise of all the food she and the children would need from Nellie and the members of the Christian Women's Wednesday Circle. And Carlene, distraught when their family's only milk cow dried up and the baby was without milk, was reassured by Ella Mae that at least one pail of milk from her cows would be sent to Carlene's house each morning until Ol' Bess started producing again.

Time has not erased the memories of all the wonderful stories I heard sitting under those quilts, and I can still recall the feelings of connectedness and of safety I sensed in the presence of strong women who supported each other. At a very early age I had heard them share the most intimate details of their lives and receive comfort and nurture from each other, picking up the following week where they had left off the week before—both in their quilting and in their stories.

Although I didn't have the words as a young girl to capture this feeling of belonging, I came later to realize that this experience was elegant in its simplicity. It was many years later, when my young son snuggled in his bed each night under one of these quilts, that I fully understood. These women of my childhood were not only making beautiful quilts to warm the bodies of those they loved, they were also weaving the patterns of their lives. And mine.

23

A Little Help from My Friends

I'VE NEVER GOTTEN THIS "SPRING CLEANING" THING. I love springtime—I open my windows for the fresh air; I watch for the first buds to pop open and the first flowers to bloom. I look for the neighbors I haven't seen during the winter months to begin puttering around in their yards, fertilizing their grass that is already greener than mine, displaying new patio furniture, waving as I pass by. I'm not a spring cleaning Scrooge, I just somehow don't get around to doing any of it. The cleaning trait didn't make it onto my chromosomal chain. But maybe there's still hope for me. I'm just a late bloomer.

Years ago, when my son was a time-consuming five-year-old, a friend said that she didn't understand how I found time to do all that I was doing. "It's easy," I said. "I just made the decision that I will clean my house when my son goes to college." Five years later, when someone else made a similar comment to me, I said, "It's easy. I've decided that I will clean my house when Eric enters graduate school." My friend, who had been present when my first comment had been made, reminded me that I had said I'd get the job done when my son went to college. "I know," I reassured her, "but that's getting too close."

I suffer from the same malady where spring gardening is concerned. I have nothing close to a green thumb. When my friends notice that the pansies I bought to plant last summer—or whenever it is you're supposed to plant them—are still in the garage, dry, shriveled shadows of their former selves, I say somewhat defensively, "Listen, I'm a psychologist. I do people, I don't do plants."

Recently everyone at a table at which I sat attending a meeting was given a bulb beautifully wrapped in pink tissue paper tied with a pretty ribbon. We were assured that soon it would blossom into a beautiful flower. Mine sat wrapped in its pretty pink paper on my kitchen table for two weeks and absolutely nothing happened. Later I learned from a friend gushing about how beautiful her blossom was that you were supposed to take the bulb out of the tissue and plant it. Who knew?

I do better when I think of spring cleaning as a metaphor for one of the cycles we experience in life. For me, it is a special time of the year when I feel the urge to lighten up, to throw open the windows, and to bask in nature's great gifts of new life and new beginnings. Spring cleaning allows me to clear out some psychological cobwebs, clean up some emotional debris, allow light into some of the dark, wintry recesses of my heart and mind, and open up to new possibilities that this season represents. It is a time to do some dusting off of fears and worries, some cleaning out of mental closets filled with "dirty linen"—dark, hurtful secrets, hidden shame, sadness, and grief.

Recently my closest friend spent several hours helping me clear out my real closet, identifying things I still needed to keep, emptying shelves and hangers weighted down with items that no longer fit me, that had never really worked for me because I had picked the wrong size from the beginning but held on to them year after year, move after move, closet after closet. When we finished this task and I could actually walk into my closet, I was astonished. The space was organized, and my clothes were arranged by seasons of the year: beautiful scarves I didn't remember I had now adorned jackets, and sweaters rescued from dark cubbyholes now hung boldly in single rows, waiting to be worn and appreciated. This exercise also provided the opportunity for me to get rid of some old, painful, hurtful memories associated with the death of a dear friend several years ago, to address old sadness and grief, to let them go along with the clothes and other items that were associated with that period of my life. It allowed me to tidy up the closet of my life. I began to see some things from a fresh perspective, and to create some empty space for new aspirations, new desires, new hopes as I allowed my own personal growth-producing springtime to unfold. Letting go of old hurts, old resentments, old fears creates space for more joy, more peace, more happiness.

So, spring cleaning as a metaphor allows me to participate in the annual rite of spring. Embracing the metaphor, I can finally appreciate the value of spring cleaning. We all need to clean out some old closets, empty out some drawers, dump some old outdated files from the filing cabinet. We all can empty our emotional suitcases that have held us back or slowed us down as we have continued to drag them behind us for a long time—sometimes since childhood. Unknowingly, some of us drag that suitcase around for too many seasons without opening it up to see if it needs to be unpacked and made ready for a new season, a new journey.

What role do close friends play in our spring cleaning? Maybe there are people who can muddle through this process alone, but not me. Left to my own devices, my gardening "brown thumb" could turn black; my emotional closet could remain cluttered; my fear of swimming could have kept me shut off from a wonderful underwater world. Friends give me essential feedback that allows me to make a mid-course correction. Without them I could become defensive and less open to trying new things. But by responding to their observations and insights, by taking opportunities they provide, and by honoring their caring for me, I invite them to be part of a feedback loop that keeps me on track in my own personal growth and spring cleaning efforts.

Our friends can help us reevaluate old choices that may not be serving us well, to clean out congested areas of our lives, to travel light and dwell deep, to make space for new experiences, to go snorkeling in new waters. If we missed the opportunity last year to do this kind of internal spring cleaning, we needn't worry; our friends—and Mother Nature—will always provide us with second chances.

24

Play Fair!

PLATO SAID, "YOU CAN DISCOVER MORE ABOUT A PERSON in an hour of play than in a year of conversation." Many of us do not know the art of fair play. When we have no skills in how to play, we revert to teasing or bullying.

Each of us knows adults who do not know how to relate playfully and instead bully each other over the most insignificant things. At a recent dinner party, I observed my friends Larry and Sara. Poor Larry couldn't seem to do anything right. "Don't stack all those cups up in one stack," Sara told him. "You're going to break them!"

When guests were seated, Sara announced with a strained laugh, "Larry thinks he's a big help, but he didn't remember that the napkins go on the left side of the plate, not on it!"

Sara's endless critique went on throughout the meal. The squirming guests wondered how long Larry would remain silent. Finally, they had their answer. As dessert was being served, a guest admired the silver spoon with berries and leaves etched into it, being used as a serving tool.

Larry spoke up. "This berry spoon has been in Sara's family for several generations. It's as wide as a spatula, but it still fits in Sara's mouth." He turned to the guests and laughed.

Sara and Larry are not playing fair. This is bullying. Laughter is a good indicator of positive mental health only when it is not at the expense of someone else.

When a person is being bullied, we can try to lighten the atmosphere, try to refocus, interrupt the behavior, or reinterpret the situation. It helps if we see the bully as insecure and limited in coping skills. Often, in severe cases, there is some kind of abuse or neglect behind the behavior.

Learning to play fair with others and knowing what is a clean fight are things we all have to work on. The tendency to bully is part of our lower human nature. There are times when we all resort to brute force—or wish we could. But because human beings are not brute animals, we can transcend bullying behavior. We need to broaden our options.

My son was eight when a new kid moved into the neighborhood. A foster child, Scott was highly suspicious and guarded. When he came into our yard to play he brought toy guns and rifles. He only wanted to play war games. I told him that at our house we didn't care much for guns and rifles, but that if he wanted to play with my son, we would teach him other fun games. Scott agreed, and the guns were laid aside. At the end of the afternoon the boys had played several games and had a great time.

Adults need to start early to teach children how to play, and the best way is to begin early to play with them. "You're going to love it!" said my son—ten by then—as he handed me my Mother's Day present. I took the ribbon off a loosely wrapped, strangely shaped package. It was a baseball glove. "Are you surprised?" he asked. I was.

"Now when we play pitch and I throw the ball really hard, it won't hurt your hands."

"This is the best present!" I said. "Let's go outside and try it out."

"Okay," he said. "Next Mother's Day I'm getting you a football!"

It does not take money or privilege to be joyful and playful with a child. Bethany is a teenager whose mother was in prison when she was born. In spite of her most difficult circumstances, Bethany has managed to graduate high school and get an associate's degree. Still under twenty-one, she has had one child and is expecting another.

What touches my heart is seeing what a connected, playful mother Bethany is with her baby daughter. She has loved and cared for children from an early age, and has studied early childhood education. During a recent visit, Bethany was on the floor with her daughter, and as she spoke with me, her attention was on the child. They played together, and I noticed the twinkle in the child's eyes and the love of play that Bethany, with limited resources, has been able to give her. I left, happy in the knowledge that this child will have more security and joy than her mother had.

Much of our play is highly competitive. Competition in and of itself does not have to be negative. We need to know how to function in a competitive world. One has only to visit a Little League baseball game or some other sport in which young children are participating to see what can happen when the win-at-all-costs approach takes over and parents begin berating the coaches, criticizing the players, and modeling the worst in competitive behavior. When this happens, the value of play—the game—is lost. We *do* want to win, and winning should not be diminished, but the game needs to be put into perspective: team spirit and sportsmanship count; respectful communication and camaraderie count; doing one's best counts.

We have many opportunities to work on this issue and to embrace the values of fair play. Think about the fairy tale "Beauty and the Beast": we are all both. But we can learn to restrain the beastly side of ourselves through healthy play. In the absence of such learning, many children are turning out to be "beasts." All it takes to model fair play—and prevent that outcome—is time and caring. Try it. I d-double dare you!

25

Different, Yet the Same

"ONE OF THESE THINGS IS NOT LIKE THE OTHERS / One of these things just doesn't belong. . . ." The Sesame Street song teaches children early about similarities and differences. It seems a benign and useful skill when applied to "things," but as a concept we use in shaping our identities as persons, it can lead to dark places. It is an important concept we use in understanding who we are and who we belong to.

We naturally long for a community where we are not different—where we belong. Along the way, we all run into situations that make us feel different; it is part of the human experience. The problem is that some kinds of differences inspire fear and discomfort. That's because we fail to honor and accept differences, and instead place value judgments on them. And our culture has helped us identify and label groups of people to judge, to set ourselves apart from, be fearful of, to give thanks that we are not like "those people": gays, minorities, religious groups, those with disabilities, nerds—the list goes on and on.

Catherine McCall, a North Carolina psychiatrist and author of *Lifeguarding: A Memoir of Secrets, Swimming, and the South*, writes eloquently about what it means to be different. She shares with the reader what it is like to discover that she is lesbian, to act on that awareness, and to deal with the stress the discovery placed upon her and her family. In her review of the book, author Virginia Holman says McCall's "personal story serves to remind us that confronting our fears, that blind underwater struggle, is always worth the effort." Often, saying "I'm not like . . ." can be translated as "I'm better than . . . ." It is a defensive reaction we use to avoid feelings of fear or inferiority. The Pharisee of biblical times went to the temple and prayed, "God, I thank You that I am not like other people."

Over the years, I have witnessed the struggle of many people who are "different." I have heard stories of shame and guilt, of anger and sadness, of resentment and frustration. Many members of minority groups told me that they equated being different with being deficient. With this internalized view of themselves, they felt compelled to be perfect, to be the best, to compensate for their "deficiency."

In 1955, Veda Wilson was nine years old, living with her parents in an all-black neighborhood in Washington, D.C. Her family was the only one on the block with a television set, and Veda had seen an advertisement on it for a local amusement park. She asked her mother if they could go, and her mother said no.

"Why not?" Veda asked.

"Because they don't allow colored people there," her mother answered.

Veda says this was the first time she knew about so-called colored people and that there was a part of life that she could not participate in because she was "colored."

The next year, Veda's family moved to an almost all-white neighborhood so their bright daughter could go to a good school. Veda told me, "The first day of elementary school I learned that there were 'A' classes and 'B' classes. 'A' classes were for the brighter, quicker kids, and 'B' classes were for the rest. I went from being the top of my class to being placed in 4B, along with the other two 'colored girls,' Beverly Haynes and Shirley Jackson.

"The first spelling test had the word 'microscopic' in it and I thought, *I'm in big trouble; I've never even heard of this word, never mind knowing how to spell it.*" Veda went home and told her mother this story.

"I don't know what it means, either," her mother said, "but you have a set of World Book encyclopedias, so go look it up." Her parents had bought her the books on installment. She looked up the word and began reading the encyclopedias.

"That was the last time I was afraid in that class. The next year the 'three colored girls' were in 5A," Veda says. She doesn't know what happened to one of their school trio, but Veda is a retired senior foreign service officer in the U.S. Diplomatic Corps, and the other earned a Ph.D. in physics from MIT and is now a college president.

Coming to terms with being different begins with the inside process of accepting yourself, followed by learning how to negotiate how you will live in a society that holds different and often hostile views. Once this happens, there is a kind of joy that comes from being free of convention.

How can we help our children cope with being different? How can we teach them to value and embrace diversity? It always starts with ourselves. Parents can provide a safe environment where differences are openly discussed. As parents and caring adults, we can model acceptance and value the diverse human community. We can find common ground. We can model curiosity, not fear. We can have fun exploring and learning about other cultures. We can help shatter stereotypes and hold up the worth of all people.

When the fear of differences controls us, everyone in the situation loses. It is always possible to transcend dark aspects of our nature and to see the beauty of uniqueness, to learn from it, and, in the final analysis, to see that in many important ways we are all the same. The saints of old have taught us that with the seed of love planted in our hearts—despite all our differences—a feeling of oneness is brought about and grows within us.

26

Travel Light, Dwell Deep

MY MOST MEMORABLE "SUMMER" VACATION happened in February when my friend Louise hatched an exciting plan that would take us to Isla Mujeres, Mexico.

Shortly before our flight landed in Cancun, she took out an envelope containing a note, a key, and Mexican money: she had rented a house at a bargain price from her brother's close friend, and he had sent her a key along with cash to pay the caretaker of the house. We could barely contain our glee as I read aloud from the travel brochure: "Isla Mujeres, the Island of Women, where time passes slowly and your dream vacation becomes a reality."

The ferry ride took us from Cancun to Isla. From the dock we took a taxi to our home for the week. Three miles outside the village we pulled up to a tiny whitewashed hacienda, partially hidden by palm trees and bougainvillea.

Louise paid the taxi driver, after arranging for him to wait for us to freshen up and then to take us back into town for dinner. She reached in her purse for the envelope with the key. It wasn't there! She quickly realized she had left the envelope on the plane.

"Put on this hat and wait here," she said. "I'm going down the road to find the caretaker. Surely he has a key." The driver and I stood in silence. He spoke no English, and I didn't trust my sparse Spanish vocabulary. Within a few minutes, she returned with a key. She was smiling. No problem.

We went inside and took quick stock of the accommodations: one bedroom, a bath, and porch upstairs for me; one bedroom, a bath, and kitchen downstairs for her. Deciding not to shower and keep the driver waiting, we changed into shorts and sleeveless shirts and headed back into town.

We ate our first meal barefoot on a sandy beach. We sat at a plastic table and enjoyed fresh fish, rice, a cool drink, a magnificent view of the sunset, and then a starry night. We laughed about the no-key incident and made light of having to reimburse the caretaker from our funds since we had lost the money that had been sent.

I awakened the next morning to the sound of Louise speaking Spanish with a stranger in the yard below my window. She was near the cistern, telling the caretaker that we had no water! I thought he was saying, "Paco usually comes by on Tuesdays and fills up the cistern." Today was Monday. He went to get a small water hose to put a few gallons from his well into our cistern so we could flush the toilets and wash our faces. Water for drinking and cooking was in a five-gallon jug on the countertop. We started to fix breakfast, happy that showers would come tomorrow—if Paco showed up.

We made mugs of strong, black Isla coffee. When it came time to make toast we discovered that the toaster did not work, nor did the broiler! Chunks of sweet butter spread on dark brown bread became Isla toast. We ate, watching a small lizard playing on the screen inside our window, and headed for a day at the beach.

The next day, water poured from the faucets, and we enjoyed our showers before heading off to meet the Mayan fisherman who had offered his small wooden boat to take us and four others to the nearby island of Contoy, a national nature preserve. We paid the captain and boarded the boat. An hour later we were anchored off Contoy, where we swam and snorkeled. We were assured that the necessary arrangements had been made for this visit, so it came as a surprise when we were pulled over by the park rangers and taken ashore to be questioned. Seems our "captain" had *not* made the necessary arrangements, and had been fishing in restricted waters. We were being detained until matters could be clarified.

"Well, Leen, have you ever been arrested before?" Louise asked with a grin. "I told you this trip would be memorable." Finally, after she paid thirty dollars to "ransom" us, we were cleared to leave the island, and our little boat returned to Isla. A small dockside restaurant prepared the illegal fish the captain had caught in restricted waters and served it with rice and beans. To keep the touristas happy, the captain arranged for us to eat free, except for drinks.

Before leaving, friends had given us two crisp twenty-dollar bills, instructing us to find the best margarita on the island. We were only too happy to comply. We eagerly sampled the house special but found it too strong and bitter. For a second round, Louise instructed the waiter in Spanish to make our margaritas sweeter. It took only two sips before my nose started to itch and my lips to feel paralyzed. After sip number three, we figured out that "make it sweeter" had been translated by our waiter as "add extra tequila." We realized what was happening and stopped sipping, but by then it was too late. Louise looked at me, wrinkling her nose and massaging her lips. "Leen, I think we have to keep looking for the perfect margarita—this isn't it!" It was late into the evening, back at our place, before our giggling subsided.

The next morning, after breakfast of coffee and "Isla toast," Louise went to take a shower. A few minutes passed before she exclaimed with dismay and a few choice words, "There's no water!"

I went to the bathroom door and found her lying in a semi-fetal position in the shower stall, her entire body lathered with shampoo and soap. The faucet refused to give up a single drop. I went downstairs to get some drinking water from our five-gallon jug. I managed to get about a quart of water into a small pitcher to take up to her.

"Where do you want this?" I asked as I squatted on the floor beside her distraught, limp body.

"It doesn't matter; just pour it anywhere," she muttered. I ceremoniously poured the water over her head, shaking the very last drop from the pitcher. She stood up and looked at her gooey hair in the mirror, and we both broke into gales of laughter. We'd head for our favorite beach, we decided. Today would be a good day for snorkeling. With any luck, fish wouldn't die from soap poisoning!

As we climbed into our snorkel gear, I said to her, "So, seeing that everyone else on the island has state-of-the-art water, what's with your brother recommending this house to you? Didn't he like you?"

She laughed. "Come to think of it, I didn't tell you earlier that the guy who owns this house was an accused criminal my attorney brother had defended."

We recently returned from our tenth vacation to this beautiful, unspoiled island. Each year we declare *that* visit to be the best ever, as Isla has become our winter vacation "home." But in my heart of hearts I secretly compare these vacations where water is available, where we visit Contoy without getting arrested, good margaritas are easily found, and keys don't get lost, with our first visit. Some travelers would consider that initial experience a lesson in adversity. We somehow didn't see it that way. Maybe we were just having too much fun to notice.

27

Party Time

THE QUESTION READ: "AT A LARGE PARTY, would you be most likely to introduce yourself or to introduce someone else?" I thought for a moment and then replied, "At a large party, I would most likely not be there."

Parties are not always treasured experiences. Some of us like to receive lots of invitations because we can be reassured that we are regularly active in the social loop. Others dread having to RSVP and dread even more having to reciprocate. Some get paralyzed with fear and anxiety at the thought of walking into a room full of people. Others medicate themselves in order to be able to show up and participate. And of course there are those who begin to tank up on alcohol as soon as they arrive at the party. Holiday parties can be nightmares for families with alcohol problems.

That opening question posed to me was part of a questionnaire designed to determine whether I am extroverted or introverted. The introvert supposedly would introduce herself, and the extrovert would introduce others who had quickly become acquaintances or buddies. Even introverts can feel lonely and left out if others get invitations to notable parties and they don't. However, getting such an invitation feels like a hot potato: *I need to be wanted,* we might think, *but don't make me go.*

The fear of being left out, unwanted, unloved, can pressure us into very uncomfortable situations. We need to be able to keep social life in balance so that we aren't stressed out and exhausted. If your life is stressful, big parties you throw or feel obligated to attend have the potential for adding more stress. Holidays and major life events such as weddings are good times to remind ourselves of the need to have our lives in balance.

Using our social life to escape the stresses of daily living can be costly. If we need to tally up our invitations, if we believe that if we are invited to such-and-such an event then we are *somebody,* then we expect too much from the event and risk disappointment. How can we make parties fun and enjoyable? How can we participate in events that are important parts of life and feel our energy renewed and our emotional health nurtured?

The best social events for me are those where no score card is kept and no strings are attached to the invitation. There is no obligation to reciprocate.

I have two extroverted friends who throw their own big birthday party each year, opening their home to friends and acquaintances. Crowds throng to enjoy delicious homemade delicacies and to delight in clever themes and decorations.

On the other hand, knowing myself to be an introvert, I'm aware that I benefit from small groups. On some Christmas Eves, I have had a brunch and open house that is easy to prepare for and registers very low on the stress meter. My closest friends know that I am not a good cook. So brunch works for me and protects them. What can go wrong with bagels and fresh fruit?

Parties that come out of a sense of obligation, that fill the planner and the invited guest with dread and a desire to get it all over with quickly, should be avoided whenever possible. What are some creative ways around this? Taking early inventory concerning plans and expectations is important. Identify those parties that feel obligatory and have a plan for dealing with them. If your spouse's career *truly* depends on your showing up at the office party, you and your partner need a heart-to-heart talk before the event to decide what degrees of freedom you have in the situation. It is helpful to take time to get in touch with what you most need from the event and how that need can be met.

One introverted friend has always shied away from events involving large numbers of people. This year she is expecting her daughter, son-in-law, and new grandchild for an extended holiday visit. Her daughter is an extrovert who loves having groups of people around. My friend is energized by this possibility and is looking forward to it. But she is already asking herself what support she will need to host several events, and how she can be sure her own needs will be met within this newly defined role. She will talk with her family and close friends, asking for their help and support. With a little awareness and a little effort, introverts and extroverts can understand each other and can find genuine comfort levels in accommodating each other's needs.

A social life that satisfies us enhances life. We need to be aware that traditions can be changed; activities can be modified or refocused. If the situation is not going to change, then *we* need to. We can do this by making adaptations or accommodations, by making a shift in our attitude or mindset. Feelings matter. We need to respect genuine comfort levels and to honor them. What is unhealthy is to go round and round year after year with the same dread that wells up with the first holiday display or the arrival of the obligatory graduation or baby shower invitation. Parties can be great fun if the party and the party-goer are good matches.

Whether the occasion is formal or informal, work-related or with family or friends, whether we're an invited guest or the host, knowing what we can bring of ourselves to these occasions means that we do not have to arrive—or leave—feeling psychologically empty-handed. It's not about eliminating social events to our calendar, or adding them. It's about finding a comfort level, a balance that allows us to participate and enjoy what is essential *to us,* and from that perspective to be able to embrace and enjoy our lives.

28

Let's Get to Broadenin'

"WELL, WE KNOW THAT BIRDS DON'T SING the same songs," my eighty-three-year-old friend, Ma Barefoot, said in her offhand way when I told her what this essay was going to be about: enlarging our perspective on the world by getting to know different people around us. How many times have I seen her eyes dancing and her hands clapping as she delights in some new experience. "My world is broadenin'," she says.

Every culture has traditions regarding the seasons. In the South we eat black-eyed peas and hog jowl on New Year's day to bring us good luck for the year. Once we enlarge our world, study other cultures, and take everyone into account, we discover that while every culture celebrates a new year, the dates may differ, along with the words and the foods for good luck. What is universal is the joyous celebration of life renewing itself.

However we view creation, we know that nature loves variety. This can be seen everywhere, from skin color to beautiful gardens laden with blossoms. "There are so many colors in the rainbow / so many colors in the morning sun / There are so many colors in the flower / and I see every one," sang Harry Chapin. I believe that the more "colors" we can appreciate, the more respect we have for variety, the more we are rewarded with meaningful, joyful lives.

As we expand our definitions of traditional and non-traditional, as we strive towards non-judgmental, non-prejudicial approaches to relationships, we can hold out the hope that the values we share in common outweigh our differences, allowing us to support fidelity and commitment in relationships. Perhaps we can then create new terms and definitions which embrace the assumption of inclusiveness. We can honor the love story that is creation.

Philip Stine and Veda Wilson, an interracial couple who moved to my neighborhood in 1999, have been married for many decades. They met in 1974 while each was working in Nigeria. Veda was an assistant branch public affairs officer in the U.S. Diplomatic Corps, and Philip was a trainer of translators for the United Bible Societies. "One day we heard that there was a single American woman at the Consulate, so we all went over," Philip said with a laugh and a twinkle in his eye.

"Every day for two weeks a different American or Brit would show up at my door," Veda said. "Philip arrived in outlandish shorts and an unbuttoned shirt. That was eye-catching." Two years later she and Philip were married on the Ivory Coast and honeymooned in Kenya and Tangiers.

Philip lived much of his life in Africa. In the mid-1980s he took on global responsibilities from his offices in New York, traveling more than 150,000 miles a year. Veda, too, had several different assignments with the Diplomatic Corps that took her to several foreign countries.

For eleven of their years together they didn't live in the same country, but they made an effort to see each other at least one weekend a month. While Veda was posted in Brussels, Belgium, Philip moved there to be with her and joined a group who followed their career spouses, that they called STUDS: Spouses Trailing under Duress Successfully. This group received international news coverage. Philip has his engraved STUDS mug to remind him of this experience.

Veda and Philip have traveled the globe and lived in many different places. What brought them to a small city in North Carolina to retire? Veda wanted to end her career before 2000 and wanted to live in a warm climate. She and Philip wanted a university town, the ocean, and an airport, all within easy driving to Washington, D.C., where Veda grew up and still has family. "When we decided to look at Wilmington we told the real estate agent that we were a racially mixed couple and we didn't want to live where crosses would be burned on our front lawn," Veda says. "The realtor assured us that this would not be a problem in Wilmington. It hasn't been."

As a couple they have experienced no prejudice or bias, though, as Veda notes, "We do stick in people's minds as a couple. When we enter a restaurant there's always a fork in someone's hand that stops in midair." Veda smiles. "We are not noticed as individuals but as a couple."

Since retiring as a senior foreign service officer, Veda undertook acting in locally filmed movies and in community theater productions, serving on civic, nonprofit, and university boards, and participating in the local chapter of a sorority for public service.

Philip, with a Ph.D. in linguistics and postdoctoral work in biblical studies, spent years with United Bible Societies, training translators, before leaving in 1998. Known internationally for his scholarly work, he now is consulting in international publishing and marketing, assisting groups in developing marketing strategies. He also holds the distinction of being the only male board member on the county's Commission for Women.

What has been most important in making an interracial marriage work? The couple point to several factors. For one, much of their married life was spent overseas, where they found less prejudice towards interracial couples. Philip's background enables him to be comfortable being the "only white guy" in certain situations—his "stag" party on the Ivory Coast the night before marrying Veda was attended only by women! Veda's experiences in the Diplomatic Corps allow her to be comfortable in a white society. She adds, "We developed an attitude that if someone objects to our marriage, it's their problem." Their marriage works, they believe, because they don't worry about what they *don't* have in common.

"We respect each other's independence," Veda explains. Philip attributes the marriage's success at least in part to the fact that they show each other courtesy and respect and that they guard their own individual identities.

Getting to know Philip and Veda reminds us to value intimate relationships and to honor those who live dedicated, committed lives. Philip and Veda are full of the energy and good humor life brings as we go about meeting our needs for self-awareness, for belonging, for connectedness, for understanding, for being loved. Their world is ever broadenin'!

29

Connectile Dysfunction

"WITHOUT FRIENDS, YOU FARE TOUGH," my friend Mary is fond of saying. She's right. Community and friends are important to us because we need a context within which we say, *I exist; I'm here.* When we leave the homes we were raised in and move into an ever-expanding world, our perceptions change. What are we to make of it all? There are many possible responses to this universal experience: disillusionment; fear of the unfamiliar; curiosity to know more. There is the tension of wanting to retreat to safety and wanting the thrill of moving into a new adventure. Our community and our friends can help us feel connected and grounded instead of fearful and overwhelmed.

To answer the question of how important community is, we need look no further than the tragic school shootings that have horrified the world in recent years. In each case, the killer's mental illness prevented him from feeling a part of a community. Without that feeling of belonging and having a stake in the well-being of others, a person lacks empathy and feels disconnected.

The chief characteristics of mental illness are withdrawal and isolation. Without a community, we suffer from what one cellular telephone ad calls "connectile dysfunction." It is a syndrome ignored at great peril. Lacking that essential feeling of connection, many of our young people go up in flames, sometimes taking others with them.

For me, the inability to connect and feel valued in community is diagnostic for depression and suicide. As a clinical psychologist, I spent twenty years—first in a mental health center, and later in a large school system—evaluating *hundreds* of young people who were at risk for suicide. I came to see that the strongest predictor of immediate threat of suicide was whether or not the teenager had a support system—a community. Being in community lowered the risk; a feeling of having no support system increased the immediate danger. Identifying and putting in place a supportive community for the individual became my first step in intervention. Often, when there was no support readily available, I temporarily became the teenager's "community."

"I've tried everything and nothing works," suicidal clients often said to me.

"It may feel that way, but I don't believe that's true," I would respond.

"What do you mean?"

"Well, you haven't tried talking to me," I'd say. "I can't stop you if you decide you want to die, but since there is such a degree of finality to suicide, maybe you want to wait and see if I can help."

"How long is it going to take for me to feel better?" my young clients often asked.

"I can't say for sure," I might respond, "but I need you to promise me that you will give us a chance. I'd hate to have to say to people, 'You know, I knew this really cool kid in a lot of pain but with a bright future, but she checked out on me before we had a chance to see if we could fix things.' Will you promise me that you'll hang in there?" In twenty years, *no one* ever turned down my offer, and *no one* among this very large group I worked with committed suicide. Even a community of one has great power.

We spend relatively little time in our family of origin and most of our lifespan elsewhere, working out the issues formed in and by our early experiences. It is never too late to create a healthy community for yourself. Don't let community happen without you. Know who you are and find a community that is compatible. If you know who you are and the community you're in at work or at home doesn't make you happy—if it brings dread and fear—move on. Decide what you want; don't wait; reach out for it. After you are secure in a community, be sure to reach out to the lonely, the isolated, and help them find a support system, too.

Human beings bond for safety, learning, transition from family, celebration, mutual aid, comfort, fun. Belonging needs come right after the need for food and shelter. Healthy adjustment includes connection to the natural world and feeling part of the human race. The ultimate payoff is feeling connected even when we are alone. We can identify ourselves with a wider, intangible community. We can feel pleasure through noticing the beauty around us.

I like belonging to groups that hold me to account. It doesn't mean that I always get my way, but within a communal framework I can both give and take comfort. And, when I go astray, the group helps me make a midcourse correction.

Life is hard—at best. We need to learn how to create a community that allows our heart to sing, despite the challenges and losses we must face. Connections give us the courage to go forward, through fear, tension, and stress, knowing we are all in this together.

lesson five

The Knack of Being Happy with Dating, Mating, and Marriage

Love is the soul's life,

Love is simply creation's greatest joy.

. . .

I caught the happy virus last night
When I was out singing beneath the stars.
It is remarkably contagious—
So kiss me.

—HAFIZ

Here's the deal about relationships: Where there is one, there is an opinion; where there are two, conflict will appear. When there are three, there is resolution. Renowned psychologist Carl Jung says where there is one, the opposite will appear, often with conflict. What is needed is a third entity.

What is this third entity? In dating, mating, and marriage, it is the claim of the relationship itself. The question is not what is good for you versus what is good for me, but what is good for the relationship. If we think in these terms, we understand that in dating and mating relationships, our task is to retain our individual integrity without subverting the relationship or disregarding the other person.

When it comes to dating, we must be careful to avoid attaching our weakness to another person's imagined strengths, expecting that person to sustain us. Many people just wait for a relationship to come along instead of taking action to make things happen.

For years my young, very shy friend had wanted to meet women but had not been comfortable putting himself out there. Instead, he accepted a date only if a friend or relative introduced him to a young woman. Finally, he told me that waiting for girls to appear on your doorsteps just didn't work, and that going out with people your family and friends set you up with wasn't working for him either. So, he, like so many young people today, checked out a dating service, went through the interview process, filled out reams of questionnaires, had his picture taken and his background checked, and paid his money for the service. Within days he had had two dates, and within weeks four more. In the process he learned something about himself, gained some assurance about dating, and began to discern what it was he wanted in a relationship. Out of this process, he and a young woman have committed to an exclusive relationship.

There is a very regressive pull in dating, mating, and marriage. There is a tendency to reach deep back into the past—to the family of origin for values and patterns and expectations for ourselves and our mates.

It's natural to look back as we go forward, searching for someone we want to be with. But as long as we zigzag between unconscious claims and fears of our past, we are bound to make a lot of mistakes along the way. In our culture we tend to take a long time in dating to sort all this out. Speeding up the process often is not a good idea.

Just as water seeks its own level, if you want to find the right mate, be the right individual. Make choices that help you become the kind of person you would want to meet. It is more important to be the right person than to find the right person. Once you know and get along with yourself, the pool of possibilities is suddenly quite rich.

30

Matchmaking

"MATCHMAKER, MATCHMAKER, MAKE ME A MATCH, find me a find, catch me a catch," Hodel sings in *Fiddler on the Roof.* Arranged marriages have a long tradition, persisting everywhere traditional cultures thrive. When I visited India I met Ravi Shinde, a man in his twenties who had assumed head of household status because he was the only one in his family who had a job. In his position, he was responsible for finding a suitable husband for his sister. Today, even among India's former "untouchable caste," I found educated but traditional families turning to the Internet for help in this selection process.

In the United States, we have such a mix of cultures that even here we have families arranging marriages, or at least playing a pivotal role. And an increasing number of people are using dating services that bear similarities to traditional practices in that they introduce a third party into the matchmaking mix. The difference is the family has the family's interest at heart; dating services are driven by the profit motive. Each can play a useful role in the dating game if the family relationships are healthy, or if the person using the dating services is aware of possible pitfalls.

"I decided to try one of those dating services," my forty-six-year-old friend said after her marriage ended. "I filled out the questionnaires, and I found myself interested in a man I was matched with. At our first meeting, he confessed that he was ten years older than he had reported on his application. That deception was almost a deal-breaker." While he defended himself by saying he thought she wouldn't go out with him if he didn't say he was near her own age, the issue for her was honesty.

Another friend, responding to my research on this topic, was very enthusiastic: "If you want to know more about the questionnaires and how matches are identified, just go online, fill out the forms and see how you're profiled. Just make stuff up!"

"That's exactly my point!" I replied. "Maybe 'matches' are only as successful as the honesty shown by those who fill out the application."

Julie and Adam met through a dating service and have been in an exclusive relationship for almost a year. Adam, a busy computer programmer, liked the fact that all the work was done for him. He was given the first name of the person, the time and place they were to meet, and instructions that the first meeting should be short and that they should each pay for their own meal. They are among those satisfied with the service, and they attribute the good match in part to their age (both are in their late thirties) and their honesty in completing the questionnaire.

In general, men are more satisfied with the matches made through dating services, because more women than men use the services, and therefore, men have a much bigger pool to choose from. Because eligible men are harder to come by, sometimes these services are said to give preferential treatment to them.

Women often get fewer matches and sometimes are matched with men they have little in common with. One woman I know lamented, "I was paired with one man who was old enough to be my father. Turns out the only thing we could find we had in common was that we each had a dog!" According to industry insiders posting on the Internet, people who work at some of these services report being uncomfortable with the assurances they are expected to give to women about the pool of eligible men out there waiting to hear from them.

The matchmaking industry offers general matchmaking, as well as specialized services, including at least one that "helps people meet their spiritual needs." MyCountryMatch.com states that their service is "dedicated to matching down-to-earth singles with country values." And, if you are "over forty," you can "look for romance or love" at Senior Friend Finder. In the matchmaking world, "over forty" seems to put one in the "senior" category! There is even a Web site for adulterers seeking dates. Mercy! As with any profit industry, there is always the potential for abuse or base motives—some services appeal to the more dangerous or unflattering aspects of human desire, so be wise. Seeking help in finding a mate is not a bad idea. But using dating services poses risks, along with benefits. Following a few simple rules will increase the probability of success in your search:

- Decide on a financial budget. Almost all major Internet dating services charge something, often in the form of monthly or annual fees.
- Ask friends and acquaintances for recommendations.
- Research the sites; try to discover if there have been any consumer complaints.
- Take advantage of free trials; in other words, try before you buy.

In America, we are not so different from countries where arranged marriages have a long tradition. But, in this country, we have more individual responsibility for our choices. So—buyer beware!

31

Let the Good Times Roll

"My brother would never remember my birthday if I didn't remind him each year," my young friend said. "That's pretty appalling, since we're twins."

Another friend said, "My husband hasn't given me a card or a present in more than twenty years. I let him off the hook about remembering dates and rushing out to shop. I think that's more of a 'woman thing.'"

Her husband agreed. "Men don't seem to be hard-wired to get excited about giving presents; it somehow doesn't register."

Women may have a stronger pull to noting milestones—significant events—as they occur. Certainly popular Western culture supports the stereotype of the Dagwood/Hagar/Archie Bunker who forgets an important milestone, and his woman who complains about it. I don't think we know how much nature and nurture contribute to one's attachment to marking milestones with cards and gifts. But I do know that expecting other people to feel about an occasion as we do can lead to frustration and resentment.

We need to show a little compassion when important people in our lives do not value a particular holiday, birthday, or anniversary the same way we do. The key to enjoying the day itself is to make conscious choices in one's own best interest, and then let others do it their way.

For example, my friend who doesn't expect her husband to remember anniversaries is an introverted, shy, intuitive thinker. Her focus is internal, and she has zero interest in sentimentality. She does not seek external validation of her inner awareness, so Hallmark makes no money off her. Her daughter, on the other hand, is an extrovert who loves celebrating occasions with large groups of people. She enjoys getting lots of gifts, giving just the right thing to others, and attending lavish, colorful, exciting parties to note special occasions. Neither judges, criticizes, or expects the other to be different.

It helps to get to the place where you can take care of yourself. A client used to complain that her husband never remembered her birthday or their anniversary.

"Do you remind him a few days before the event?" I asked.

"If he can't figure out what I want, I'm most certainly not going to tell him!" she replied angrily.

"Maybe you're expecting your husband to be a mind reader," I said. "If so, this is a recipe for disaster." My client decided this expectation was something she needed to work on. After a few sessions, she told me that she had made a list of what she needed to make her happy on her birthday and anniversary—and for good measure, she threw in Valentine's Day.

"I gave the list of what I wanted to my husband, and you're not going to believe what happened. He thanked me! 'I can work with this,' he said."

Later, my client told me that after she had received four pieces of jewelry, eight boxes of Godiva chocolate, and six vases of tulips, it somehow didn't seem quite so important anymore. A need met was a need no more. They each did their part in fulfilling the fantasy. Now she had changed her perceptions, and she was ready to scale back on gifts.

If you feel dissatisfied with how someone else behaves at special times, you can ask yourself, "Am I being overtaken with advertising hype? What do I truly believe is important? Am I seeking excessive external approval? Am I using this one day to erase doubts and fears about whether I'm loved and appreciated? What is it that I *really* need to feel good about myself? Am I willing to do the work on myself it might take to sustain and nurture a healthy relationship?" When we can pose these questions and answer them honestly, we may find that we are looking for much more than a card and flowers—although those are nice!

Stress and unhappiness result when we put emphasis on one twenty-four hour period, rather than experiencing the flow of occasions as they come and go. We fare better if we remind ourselves that it's just another day to enjoy—we don't have to *create* the occasion; we do not need to control it; we do not have to force it. We can just *let* it happen. The word "participate" suggests a healthy stance. I do my "part," but let others do what works for them.

We may try to change people we love, but in reality, we can only tweak the differences at the margins. So, when you think of special occasions, think in terms of accepting responsibility for your own happiness. To the extent you can do that, you do not have to be overtaken by the frenzy of meeting expectations.

Appreciating the complex interaction of biochemistry, personality, hormones, the cultural environment, and the expressions of this mix that you cannot control, you can choose a joyful path. You can be a willing participant, doing what makes you happy. You can ask for what you want. You can be in control of yourself. You can ask yourself why you may be over-valuing *external* markers, rather than noting your own *intrinsic* values. You can see every day as a celebration of life itself. The point is to honor and celebrate—to have fun!

32

I've Got a Crush on You

"I've got a crush on you, Sweetie Pie," George Gershwin wrote. "All the day and nighttime, hear me sigh." We all have known that feeling. To be human is to be susceptible to crushes. It's in our chemistry. A crush is an intense and usually passing infatuation. However, if a crush goes on and on, it can turn into an obsession, taking up more time and energy that we can spare.

Erin, a college freshman, called her mother to tell her she had a mad crush on an older man on campus. "He doesn't know I exist," the daughter said, "but oh, Mom, he's absolutely perfect." Her mother listened, and then gave a reply I wish I had thought of: "Oh, Erin, that's so amazing! Doesn't it just suck?"

Crushes reflect developmental issues, beginning early, intensifying in adolescence, and reappearing over and over at critical times in our lives. When you think about it, crushes are perfect. We have a limited amount of information about the object of our infatuation, often information that has been carefully selected. We find this person attractive and go on to idolize him or her. Often we focus on the externals. "We both like football, we both listen to the same music, and our favorite desert is chocolate chip ice cream. How could anyone else have so much in common?" a teenager wondered.

What's the difference between a crush and true love? Some argue that there is no difference in types of love, in that all forms spring from the same human desire to connect with another human being. As a part of social and sexual development, an adolescent crush is one stage in learning how to manage that connection. However, among adults, crushes are equal parts illusion and lust, not love. Crushes meet a superficial need for excitement and variety. They put us in touch with the energizing intensity of life. For at least a while, crushes are innocent fun and they make us feel good.

"I had a crush on Jason for all my adolescence," my young friend, now in her early twenties, told me recently. "I thought he was God's gift to the world. But it was all fantasy-based," she added. "I chalk it up to hormones. He never knew how I felt, which is probably a good thing. There was no way he could have *ever* lived up to my expectations."

"How about now?" I asked.

"I still have a crush on Harrison Ford. I think he's the epitome of sexiness. I know he's older than my dad, but I don't care. I know it's all fantasy. There's no way I'll ever even meet him, but it's still fun."

It is important that we not let crushes shape our behavior—making us do things that are not in our best interest. A crush can be like a drug, if we are not careful.

"All my crushes have come from my lower self and been driven by my alligator brain," my friend said. "If you let the crush drive your behavior, everyone involved will suffer."

"My fourteen-year-old daughter paid a price because I did not see the person at church who had a crush on me as a predator," a client told me. "He was a married man who was flirtatious and I was flattered. Finally, I spoke up, told him I was happily married, and put him in his place, without any damage to me. But my daughter, then in her formative years, suffered permanent scars when he turned his attention to her in sexually inappropriate ways. I wanted to believe I was so charming that he 'fell' for me, and so I failed to see the predator below the surface."

Teenagers are especially vulnerable to crushes, which can put them in danger. A crush on an older person poses a risk for young people to be preyed upon by irresponsible adults. Well-adjusted adolescents who share open communication with parents are less at risk of being abused or taken advantage of. If adults have not resolved their own sexuality and consciously accepted their responsibility in relationships, they cannot model healthy behavior for their children. Young people fare better with adults who are aware of the power of their sexuality and have some insight and control.

Sometimes crushes do turn into mature, loving relationships. While a crush is one-sided, mature love is a process that involves meeting each other's needs. Eddie was working in a department store when he saw Flora working in an adjacent department. He developed a crush on her. He was sure she was everything he wanted and needed. She hadn't given him a moment's thought. One day he followed her onto the escalator, and by the time they reached the top, he had blurted out his feelings to her. She informed him that she thought he was crazy. They were each married, but they developed a friendship. When Flora divorced, she refused to go out with Eddie until his divorce was finalized. But eventually they did date—and now they have been happily married for more than forty years.

Crushes happen and cannot be taken back, even if they conflict with our overall preferences. Sarah developed a crush on a married man in her church. She found herself excited and desperate to get his attention. Finally, she realized that this situation was not good for her. The crush was based on pure fantasy and was so powerful that she had to take action to protect herself. She left the church, a painful choice she found was the only way to end contact with him. Crushes can be innocent if we understand what they really are. If we are overwhelmed by them, they have powerful consequences and can lead us down a destructive path.

It's not for nothing that this state of affairs is called a "crush." As a verb, "to crush" has another definition: "to damage or destroy by great weight; to defeat completely." If we let crushes drive our behavior, we may unleash that second meaning!

33

Reconnecting with a First Love

The telephone rang and the man's voice on the other end, somewhat hesitant, was vaguely familiar. "Is this the Sally Jones who graduated from Evergreen High in 1974?"

Suddenly Sally remembered. She blushed and her heart skipped a beat. "Oh, my God, Jack, it's been *years!*" She couldn't keep from wondering what her teenage heartthrob looked like—or what his life was like now. She felt as though she'd been asleep for decades and her Prince Charming had finally come to awaken her. This phenomenon—our romantic myth-fantasy—is quite common, a tribute to the power and comfort of first love.

A former flame entered Melanie's place of business years after she had married someone else, moved to another state, and reared a family. He told her he happened to be in her city and was "just checking" on her to see if she might be interested in rekindling the spark. "He just happened to be passing by my keyhole and saw that I was in," she said with a laugh. "I told him I wasn't interested, but I keep wondering about him. Do you think I should call him?"

Most often, a call like this comes out of the blue, set in motion by some occurrence that leads to the idea of looking up an old love. My friend Leslie heard from her first love, Stan, twenty years after their relationship ended. His wife had died and he had come across an old high school yearbook with their pictures under the caption "Most Likely to Succeed."

Stan wasted no time in getting to the point: "Are you still happily married?"

"I am," she said.

"Okay, I was thinking about you and just thought I'd check." It was easy for Leslie to chuckle and file the episode in her "road not taken" file, because she *was* happily married. For some who find themselves in an unhappy place when the call comes, the temptation is greater. Those who fear that life is passing them by may act on the impulse to try to connect with a happier past. Others see the pitfalls and resist.

Sometimes when love calls, it's better to just hang up. That is the advice Dr. Nancy Kalish, writing in *Psychology Today,* gives to a married person who gets a call from a long-lost lover. If the married party begins a dialogue, she cautions, "it usually breaks up a marriage. Someone is going to get hurt." According to Kalish, when such renewed contact doesn't result in marital dissolution, it often leads to adultery. About one-fourth of lost-love relationships are extramarital.

The Internet can locate almost anyone. Google makes it possible for us to check out our fantasies, but sometimes with disastrous results. A rekindled romance can happen at any age, but middle age puts many at risk for this kind of behavior. When we reach that place in life, we often reexamine our marriage or primary relationships. We see our children leaving the nest and feel incredibly lonely. We agonize over unfulfilled dreams and aspirations. We begin to feel old, and not at all the person we thought we would be. Inner pressure can drive us in unhealthy directions. This passage is a time when it is hard to take responsibility for our lives, but it is also a time to remember that we can choose to create a legacy we can be proud to leave our loved ones.

One of the many fantasies about avoiding middle age is embodied in the dream of returning to our high school class reunion and finding our long-lost sweetheart there, still waiting for us! Anxiety about such a reunion revs up emotional intensity and heightens a sense of sentimentality. After all, this is the person with whom we shared a frog soaked in formaldehyde in high school biology lab. What could be more romantic than that?

When we are adrift, when our inner roots are not deep, fantasies take over. Sometimes the "first love" itself was a fantasy, and reconnecting with an unrealized dream or unrequited love means adding fantasy upon fantasy. Two fantasies do not make a reality. If you can resist, most often you will be better off not to act on the fantasy, even if you locate the person. If you can't resist, be prepared for the risks involved. Fantasies have a way of not holding up.

There are times, however, when reconnecting to an old love *does* work. Linda, approaching age sixty, had been divorced for twenty years and had built a successful business. One day she came across some information that reminded her of Jim, the great love of her life. She had been in her twenties; he was joining the military and refused to begin married life with her when he might not return from a long tour of duty in Vietnam. While he was far away, she found someone else and married. Jim continued a successful military career.

More than thirty years later, Linda found him on the Internet and learned that he had been a widower for several years. When they reunited and picked up where they had left off, they brought to the romance years of happy relationships with others, successful business ventures and financial security, and a maturity and wisdom that has now paid off in a rich life together. They did not come to each other encumbered by secrecy, dishonesty, or infidelity. This was a clean deal. When couples like Linda and Jim reunite, they have a very high "stay-together" rate.

"No one understands how intense these relationships are," Kalish warns. "People think they can simply reminisce with an old lover. But it's a very powerful experience and they can't get out." The source of this power has to do with romantic myth-fantasies and the importance of early experiences in shaping our later love ideals.

Getting older does funny things to us. Sometimes it leaves us anxious, dissatisfied, restless, vulnerable to remorse about "what might have been." But we have choices. We can indulge the fantasy, drink in the intoxication of the risk, or take an honest look at our situation and accept life as it really is. Returning to an old love *can* be a wonderful thing with a happy ending, but this does not happen often. Knowing this, when the call comes you have to decide whether to reconnect—or hang up.

34

Sick Relationships versus Solitude: Learning to Be Alone

LET ME SAY UP FRONT THAT ONE OF THE MOST important relationships we can ever participate in is the one we have with ourselves. When we have a good, healthy, nurturing relationship with ourselves—that is, when we can focus more on being non-judgmental about our bodies and our personalities; when we are committed to self-care; when we nourish our self-esteem; when we are not fearful about being alone—then we can bring our best, whole, integrated, growing self into a solid, meaningful relationship with others. But this doesn't come easy. The relationship with self is a process. It is a goal, the work of a lifetime. But it *is* doable. And it *is* worth the doing.

A popular song of the 1970s declared that there are "fifty ways to leave your lover," but I have observed that people can find *more* than fifty ways to stay in relationships that are not healthy for them. We remain out of inertia, fear, guilt, financial insecurity, codependency, social pressure, feeling helpless, giving up. Many of us are afraid to be alone. Sometimes we equate being "alone" with being "lonely." But we are not truly adults if we cannot appreciate the value of being alone and of being lonely at times. Loneliness is not a terminal illness, nor is it a condition to be avoided at all costs. Fear of being alone, fear that we are somehow inadequate, fear that we simply can't make it without a mate, fear of judgment and criticism can keep us in unhappy, unfulfilling, and sometimes dangerous relationships. In extreme cases, people habituated to brutality become as addicted to the intensity of fear and violence as others are addicted to alcohol or drugs.

The possibility of independence from toxic people, places, and things raises for us the question of our personal goals and strivings. Seeking our own personal freedom is one of life's ongoing tasks. It seems at times to come in stages—we revisit it over and over again. We can't take ourselves off the hook by saying, "Well, no one is truly free." It is possible to get there. The quest on this journey is for conscious self-awareness and the ability to make choices—even if perfection is not an option.

My client, Sara, explained what was sick about her marriage. "I was afraid of ending up like my mom with my hapless father, and I wanted a safe haven with someone strong and hard-working and successful—like my grandfather. It *never* crossed my mind that I could provide for myself, get a good education and a good job and pay my own way. I was afraid of my own imperfections, didn't trust my own judgment. I believed I was better off with the highest bidder."

In my own case, I was a graduate student in Boston when I said yes to the man who asked me to marry him. He was very intelligent and had five academic degrees, including a law degree and a Ph.D. in philosophy. Neither of us had dated much. Neither of us was yet comfortable in our sexuality. But I was the last single adult child in a large family, and I keenly felt the pressure to marry. The fact that I missed the highway exit for the church and almost missed my own wedding should have been a clue! It took a few years for me to accept that I had made a mistake—that I had overvalued intellect and undervalued the importance of passion, of mutual interests, of similar outlooks on what's important in life.

I was a miserable wife for a long time. It took many years for me to become conscious about how I was being used and emotionally abused. Finally, I found the courage to ask for a divorce. With that decision came the freedom to live my own life as an individual and as a single parent.

If it is important to us to maintain the illusion that we must be in a relationship to be whole, then that's where the energy will go, the energy that could be used to travel through life freely. When we are caught up in this illusion, we're not facing ourselves and life squarely. We have to grow, and it's painful.

Having a healthy relationship doesn't inoculate us against pain, but being in an unhealthy one guarantees it. Choose pain that is not part of self-destructive behavior; choose pain that leads to growth and health. It is the choosing that frees us.

Toxic relationships can exist between spouses, lovers, partners, between parents and children, between friends, or in the workplace. We can't avoid the potential for unhealthy relationships, but we can look at them as opportunities to identify our own issues. We can ask ourselves what we bring to the situation, how many degrees of freedom we have for change, what the risks and benefits are, what the cost and promise are.

There are times when people find themselves in a terrible relationship with no clearly marked exit doors. But they can access the resources they have and seek opportunities within those limits.

How do we begin? By accepting that we need a community of support. We can find someone we trust and seek guidance. Sometimes this can be a dear friend and sometimes it may need to be a professional counselor who can help us see repetitive patterns in relationships. Often choices of partners or friends are affected by many things outside our awareness. Once we become more aware, we can see if "letting go" is a good choice. We can find books on topics we need to understand better. We can keep a journal. We can bring fresh air from many sources into the picture. The more conscious awareness we can bring to the way we live and to the choices we make, the more freedom we will have. Whoever told us that "what you don't know won't hurt you" was wrong.

Contrary to many popular songs, we do *not* find ourselves in someone else. We find ourselves in our own conscious awakening, in our own search for meaning and authenticity. When we are free to bring *that* self into all our relationships, we enrich our lives beyond measure. Why settle for less?

35

Anniversaries—Ready or Not!

"TODAY IS KURT AND JANET'S WEDDING ANNIVERSARY!" The solemn evening worship service ended with the cleric's joyful announcement to those assembled. My friends Janet and Kurt looked at each other, puzzled. "It is?" they asked each other.

What the confused couple didn't know was that earlier in the day, someone had overheard Kurt say, "We can't argue today; it's our anniversary." What the listener didn't know, though, was that early into their marriage more than twenty years ago my friends had decided that they would not celebrate their anniversary just one day of the year, but they would consider each day their anniversary. That way, neither of them would ever be in trouble for forgetting the date! The congregation broke into applause and moved to the social hall, and the festivities began.

During the celebration, Janet, overcome with guilt, whispered to the wife of the minister, "I must tell you that today is *not* our anniversary." There was a moment of stunned silence, followed by a whispered, "Well, my dear, this is not the time to tell! Just enjoy!"

Anniversaries happen to us, whether we know it or not. All our holidays and special occasions are anniversaries of some sort, representing the rhythms and cycles of life. Our way of handling them is a function of our personalities and has something to do with our beliefs about life and our place within it. We greet holidays and anniversaries out of our personality structure and life experiences. Every special occasion is an occasion for getting our needs met and meeting the needs of others. If our position about life is that there is never enough, then anniversary celebrations will not be enough either! I have known people who always seem to see the glass as half empty rather than half full, and who measure each anniversary by how many people remember to call on that day. For them, there are never enough calls.

If we participate fully in the cycles of life, honoring life and death, we can see each day as an anniversary and elect to be present, sharing from a full cup. Anniversaries come to us, ready or not. Four years after his wife died tragically, Donald awakened one morning upset and irritable. On the way to work, he suddenly burst into tears. He felt like crying much of the day, and could see no reason for the upset. Finally, a friend reminded him that this day was the anniversary of his wife's untimely death. Donald did not consciously remember, but his body knew and found ways to express the unrecognized grief. Not being conscious of the date did not save Donald from the unanticipated pain.

Ignoring anniversaries such as this robs us of energy and opportunities to have options in life—to plan positive and helpful occasions for ourselves and for others. Harnessing conscious awareness turns this dynamic into a positive experience. The antidote to misery is consciousness. Do something you *decide* to do to honor and celebrate.

I recently returned from celebrating my birthday on a cruise with friends. The experience gave me a chance to reflect on how I know myself and how I handle special occasions. It allowed me to ask myself whether I am in harmony with life's rhythms, whether I am connected to things bigger than myself. My friends and I snorkeled in Turtle Bay on the island of St. Thomas, grasping each other's hands, overwhelmed with the beauty and wonder of the underwater sea life that lay before us. We visited a rain forest, walked the tiny streets of beautiful islands, basked in the tropical sun's rays, and reflected on life's ups and downs, its rhythms and cycles.

I think it all comes down to an awareness of a greater reality happening at every moment. We can deny reality, or we can choose to embrace it. Leaving my cane (which supported my broken ankle) on the sailboat, I chose to jump from the deck into the crystal-clear waters to be a part of an underwater world of beauty. I was aware of being present in the moment and of the precious gifts of the universe. What a birthday gift!

We all have choices. We can see anniversaries that happen to us without our choosing as a part of a small cycle and become twisted with fear, self-centered and out of tune. Or we can see ourselves as being in harmony with a larger, awesome cycle. We can see anniversaries not so much as a moment set in stone, but more as a drop of water in a river that is constantly flowing and changing. Maybe it helps to accept the inevitability of anniversaries and to decide to participate fully. Then every day can be an anniversary celebration of some sort.

36

Laughing Matters

"MY FATHER WAS INCREDIBLY WITTY," my client said. "He would crack jokes at the dinner table and my mother would giggle hysterically. When he wasn't there, laughter is what I missed."

Her parents were alcoholics, but she recalled the laughter and lightheartedness she experienced at the dinner table each night as "the health of our family." Humor was a quality she wanted in the man she married, but her first husband used only put-down humor that made her the butt of every joke. Her second husband has the kind of humor that is sustaining, and puts things into perspective.

"I'm not laughing *at* you," he assures her, "—I'm laughing *near* you."

Once when she was sure that everything was hopeless, especially parenting their young children, he reassured her by saying, "Let's give it another couple of days before we all join hands and jump off a cliff."

The feeling that nothing is fun—or funny—anymore is an indicator of poor mental health. That's why in my clinical practice I always paid attention to my client's sense of humor: whether he or she had one, and if so, what nature it took. I have found that humor is critical in dealing with pain, suffering, and loss.

"You don't seem to see any light at the end of your tunnel," I said to a suicidal adolescent.

"If there was any light at the end of my tunnel, it would be attached to an approaching train," she said. We both laughed. I knew then she would be able to cope.

Another client, somewhat older, chose to take a light approach as well. "I've had a mastectomy and a hysterectomy, so I have nothing left for a mid-life crisis," she said with a chuckle. "So, I think for my fiftieth birthday I'll treat myself to a colonoscopy!" It had been a tough year for her and her family, and the gentle joking provided balance and perspective.

I have worked with clients to build on a healthy sense of humor, partly because of its healing powers, and partly because I see it as a spark of the Divine that can be nurtured. Humor connects us to our spirit. "What is this precious love and laughter / Budding in our hearts? / It is the glorious sound / Of a soul waking up!" said the poet Hafiz.

Humor is one of the top traits people say they look for in a mate, but researchers do not know how important it is in making a relationship work. Sometimes one person in a relationship uses humor to avoid dealing with problems, leaving the other person feeling that the relationship is not being taken seriously. Certainly, humor alone does not make or break a relationship.

What we laugh at is an index to our character. Humor comes in more than one flavor: innocent jokes that involve word play or absurdity; humor used to reject or demean; or humor used to express power and dominance. Men seem to enjoy sexual humor more than women, who often experience it as hostile. Innocent, mirthful humor is healthy. Hurtful, demeaning humor is pathological.

The instinct for smiling and laughing is expressed early in life, suggesting its high level of importance. This instinct to play and laugh is built into us as a species. We see this in children; we sometimes forget it as adults.

Laughter is a gift to balance the suffering we all face in life. Listen to Hafiz again: "Ever since Happiness heard your name, / It has been running through the streets / Trying to find you."

While we seem to be hard-wired from birth for humor and laughter, *what* we find funny is conditioned in early childhood. Parents who respond positively to their child's budding sense of mirthful humor are building intellectual, social, and emotional skills. Some research suggest that humor supports children's self-esteem and improves mastery over anger and anxiety. "Kids who build strong humor skills prior to the adult years have a powerful advantage over their terminally serious peers when it comes to navigating daily stressors," writes Dr. Paul McGhee, an internationally known pioneer of humor research.

Mental health professionals are becoming more aware of the healing potential of humor and laughter. Evidence continues to mount that mirthful laughter reduces pain and enhances the immune and endocrine systems, thus affecting all parts of the body and reducing stress.

For several years I have participated in an exercise class of seniors that includes nonagenarian Annie. Walking slowly with her cane while the rest of us do something more strenuous, Annie keeps us laughing with her humorous observations and hilarious jokes. Her happy outlook modifies her pain, and it also adds sunshine to the aging process for all of us. We have no time for sadness or fear. Annie teaches us that no matter what our age, humor is life-affirming, interactive, and stress-reducing.

Research is now confirming what poets and sages have told us about the amazing power of humor and laughter and joy. "I am happy even before I have a reason," Hafiz says. May mirthful humor aid us in what he calls "this blessed calamity of life."

37

Never Gonna Fall for "Modern Love"

TRUE LOVE SPRINGS UP SPONTANEOUSLY and washes over us. It is always life-giving. It frequently produces tears. It cuts through our crusty hard edges and melts away the accumulated dross in our lives. True love takes care of itself if we get rid of everything that isn't truth. True love doesn't need anything from us; it's just there.

It's what allowed me to forgive the person who kidnapped, raped, and killed my sister-in-law. It's what allowed the Amish to treat the wife of the murderer of their children the same loving way they had always treated her. They chipped away at what wasn't real and embraced a truth many of us never know: true love does not have to be found. It is within us.

David Bowie once sang, "I don't believe in modern love"—the sort that's all style and no substance.

A friend said, "I am a better lover, friend and worker because I know I am deeply loved and valued. I'm not looking for love, I am looking *to* love, because I know what true love is. Knowing this, I don't have to prove anything and I don't need relationships to *provide* proof." She's right. Such demands put more stress on relationships than they can hold. It's like putting hot water in a wax jar. Sexual energy is powerful, hot stuff. It takes a strong, solid relationship to contain it.

What's modern about modern love? In a postmodern world, isn't that term already antiquated? So much happened in the late twentieth and early twenty-first centuries, and most of it plugs into walls: music videos, MP3 players, cell phones, computer dating. The trappings change so rapidly that to suggest they define love is to miss the point. It's not about the trappings; it's about the substance.

Love can surprise us. There is a physical component, but we reduce it to mere sex at our peril. Bowie compares sexual energy to "standing in the wind." Sometimes a gentle breeze, sometimes a hurricane, the wind is more powerful than we are. We may admire it, enjoy it, stand in awe of it, but we do not cause it and we can't stop it. We are fortunate if we can control it even a little bit. What we can do is respect sexuality for what it is and not invest more *personal* meaning in it than we would any other force of nature. When we look for loving companions, we are doomed to failure if we misread the source. Falling madly in love and being attracted sexually guarantees the survival of the species. It's nothing personal, it's just nature at work. Sadly, the very force that is set up to create life can also prove destructive.

With birth control freeing and separating sex from love, more women are educated, experienced, knowledgeable, strong partners in late marriages. More freedom and choices come at a high price, however. The road through them to solid ground is dangerous for the young, the insecure, the abused. Finding themselves "standing in the wind," overwhelmed by sexual disillusionment, confused about personal responsibility, feeling despair, the immature make dangerous, even tragic, choices.

Our children need the truth about love and about sexuality. They need wise old people, strong mentors, and safe communities around them as they enter adolescence. It's ironic that in our era of sexual freedom, the perilous period of adolescence can last a lot longer than in earlier times, extended as it is by the freedom to live single through years of higher education, job training, and so-called "serial monogamy."

We all need help to know the truth that we are lovable and valuable—that we can express a loving attitude in all aspects of our lives. Then we are in touch with the impersonal natural force of love that can express itself through all persons. If we are able to accept that we are loved, valued, and cherished just because we exist, then we don't require constant external validation.

Romanticism is not the "stuff" it takes to go through life. True love endures the dark. "Everyone who has a beloved pet experiences true love, whether they deserve it or not," my cat-lover friend said. "Lucy loves me when I'm impatient or cranky, when I don't pay her enough attention, when I push her away. At those times she sits at my feet, looks up at me, and starts to purr."

My advice to all who are looking for a lover in all the wrong places is to be like Lucy. Do not wait to begin expressing a loving attitude yourself. Do not be afraid to show love—there is never too much of it in the world. And don't worry about finding love: choose to be a loving, caring, joyful person and you will find people—and pets—drawn to you like moths to a flame.

Perhaps "What is true love?" is the only question worth asking. The problem is that sometimes we don't get around to asking until we're in a pickle and discover that what we thought was the real thing is anything but. We are *all* imperfect expressions of the one source. Love is the same as it always was, so don't fall for "modern"—go for the real thing.

lesson six

The Knack of a Happy Work Life

Now
That
All your worry
Has proved such an
Unlucrative
Business,
Why
Not
Find a better
Job.

—HAFIZ

Being overly identified with our work does not increase our happiness. As far as I know, no one on his or her deathbed has ever said, "I wish I had spent more time at the office." As a clinical psychologist for more than forty years, I have rarely had anyone say to me that their work is the source of their happiness and sense of self. But I have seen hundreds of people who are miserable in their work, even though they may be seen by others as highly successful.

I have seen many clients who so identified with their work that when they lost their job or they were forced to retire, they slipped into a serious depression. They had lost their identity, their sense of self. It is not uncommon to hear of someone committing suicide in the face of such loss and grief.

One distraught client told me that her work was what defined her, and that resigning before she felt ready had left her with a void that could not be filled by family or friends or her community volunteer efforts. Ignoring some serious health issues that had contributed to her earlier decision to resign, she said simply, "I have to find a job or I'm not going to be willing to stick around."

The knack of being happy in our work has to do with making decisions and taking responsibility for the decisions; it has to do with deciding to be happy despite work stress, with distinguishing between who we are and what we do, with finding balance in our lives. Good mental health, it has been suggested, involves the ability to love and to work. Finding this balance is not always easy. How do we know when we have? Joy and happiness are two of the clues.

38

Why Can't You Just Be a Teacher?

IN THE 1950S, ANY YOUNG WOMAN who graduated from high school in Roberta, Georgia, and went to college was, according to my parents, studying to be a public school teacher. Otherwise, why bother with "more learning"? So when I graduated valedictorian of my high school class and accepted a scholarship to nearby Wesleyan College, my parents knew they would have a teacher in the family. Though neither of my parents had made it beyond elementary school, they had always held teachers in high regard.

And although I was eighth of nine children, I was the first in my family to attend college. This was a *big* deal. When I announced my intentions to major in journalism, neither parent raised questions. They knew that I would be a good English teacher because I was "good with words." So sure was I of my vocational choice, I declared journalism my major in my freshman year.

At the end of my freshman year at Wesleyan, the journalism major was dropped from the curriculum. My folks assumed this was some sign from God that I would surely see. And while I did wonder if it might be some kind of omen, I didn't see it as a clear message that I should choose high school teaching as my calling. Instead, I chose psychology as my major. And from that time on, my parents professed confusion about what I really planned to do with "all that learning."

Every Saturday morning for four years my parents drove the twenty miles to the college, spending an hour or so with me and talking with my college friends. As they left, my mother gave me five dollars, my spending money for the week. Five dollars represented one-third of her weekly salary as a cook in a high school cafeteria.

There was no talk of teaching for a long while. But when graduation day arrived, my father couldn't wait to get me aside to tell me the good news. He had spoken to the chairman of the board of education in Roberta and had lined up a job for me to begin teaching tenth grade English back at my high school. And of course I could save lots of money, because I would be able to live at home.

Daddy hid his hurt and confusion when I announced that I had been accepted to graduate school at Emory University, with a scholarship and a work stipend. Mama thought this was a wonderful idea, although she made it clear she had not a clue as to what was going on. One of the things I found dearest about Mama was that even when she couldn't understand what I did, she always encouraged me to do it. Her attitude was that if *I* were doing it, then it must be the right thing to do. I was a parent myself before I fully appreciated what a wonderful gift my mother had given me: unconditional love and acceptance, the freedom to be me.

Two years later it was graduation day at Emory, and this time my father knew I had been approached to return to Wesleyan to teach psychology. If I wasn't coming home to Roberta to teach, surely I was accepting the offer to teach at my alma mater. Once again, he learned that this was not to be. I announced that I was now planning to go on for a Ph.D. in clinical psychology. And as if this weren't bad enough, "The *only* college she could pick out in the whole country," as they put it, was in Boston, Massachusetts.

My father began to accept what he could not understand, and to offer his support. That September, as I packed the little white Rambler with all my books, my hi-fi system, and my clothes, my father couldn't keep from sharing with me one last thought: as he gave me a hug he said, "I used to think you was the smartest one in the whole bunch, but it sho' is taking you a long time to learn something."

My mother kept the vigil. Years later, when I accepted a position as coordinator of psychological services and elementary guidance for the Quincy, Massachusetts, school system I was eager to show Mama my fancy stationery. The school letterhead included a two-inch border of pictures of children of all ages. Underneath the picture was my name, complete with my awe-inspiring title.

I wrote a brief note that read: "Dear Mama, How do you like my new stationery?"

"It's very nice, honey," came the reply. Then she asked the ever-present question: "Are those the students in your classroom?"

I have always had special teachers at critical points in my life. It was a teacher in elementary school who taught me the power of words and the value of speaking out about things that matter. It was a teacher who bought my first piece of luggage and clothes for college. It was a teacher who said it would "be a crime" if I did not pursue graduate work in psychology; a teacher who said, "Leen, I won't let you do that" when I considered dropping out of college for financial reasons.

It was a teacher who got me a job and a place to live when I went to Emory University; a teacher who saw to it that I received stipends for my graduate work for my doctorate and a research grant to write my dissertation. It was a high school teacher, now long retired, who mentored me for more than half a century. So I have always understood why my parents wanted me to join their ranks.

Neither of my parents was living when, many years later, I began to teach graduate courses in psychology in two different institutions, including the University of Massachusetts, Boston. I would have liked to have had the opportunity to assure my father that I had finally "learned something," and my mother that I had—at long last—made it to the classroom.

39

Creativity—Nurturing Our Vitality

It was Josh who, through his enthusiasm for Broadway musicals and live theater, taught me something special about creativity and its impact on the human spirit. Josh, an autistic child, was twelve years old when I began seeing him for twice-a-week individual therapy. He loved to sing and learned the songs from many Broadway shows. Most astonishing was how, during particularly painful times in therapy, he would recall a song that eloquently captured his feelings and would begin to sing it to me. Sometimes he would encourage me to join in.

As a severely impaired youngster, Josh had not learned the rudiments of self-care. In their love for him, his parents kept him meticulously clean and well-dressed. In one of our sessions together, Josh cried in my office, "Why can't I brush my own teeth? Why can't I splash water on my own face?"

"You can," I said. "I'll teach you." I taught Josh in painstaking detail each step in brushing his teeth. His first attempts to follow my demonstrations were less than perfect. He was nervous and dropped his toothpaste and toothbrush. He turned the water on full-force and sprayed himself and me both. Each time this happened, we would start the process over. After the fifth try, Josh had mastered the entire process. He was delighted.

The same process was repeated as I demonstrated all the steps in washing and drying his face and hands. As with teeth brushing, after several attempts he completed the process without hesitation. As we finished the session and started to leave my office Josh began humming a tune.

"What's that you're humming?" I asked.

"Right now it's one of my favorite songs," Josh said. "It's from *My Fair Lady*." He reached up and touched my face, still damp from my face-washing demonstration and sang, "I've grown accustomed to her face / She almost makes the day begin. . . ."

Josh began to take piano lessons and to enjoy plays performed by professional groups. His command of the music was impressive. When he arrived at my office to tell me with great pleasure that he had enrolled in a Boy Scout troop for special needs young men, he began to sing "I Could Have Danced All Night." We danced around the floor as Josh sang. On another occasion Josh announced that he had learned some new music and also had gotten a good report from school for improvement in behavior. This story was punctuated with a few lines from *Oklahoma*: "Everything's up to date in Kansas City; they've gone about as far as they can go." Josh looked at me. "Does this mean I've gone as far as I can go?"

"No," I said. "Maybe you're just beginning."

Later in Josh's therapy, he asked me to teach him how to use eating utensils and napkins, and how to eat in restaurants. This task was undertaken the same way that the other tasks had been approached. In my office we practiced eating with forks and spoons, drinking from a straw, reading menus, and the like. After Josh mastered this task and we had gone out to lunch a few times, he sang a few lines from *Mary Poppins*: "Come feed the birds, show them you care / And you'll be glad if you do."

As therapy was coming to an end Josh and I talked about what he had learned. Josh said, "Well, I think when I came here I was like two different boys. And I think these two boys have been put back together into one big boy. A big boy who likes himself. And since this is a very special occasion, I think I will give you a hug." After he embraced me, Josh began to hum. "This is my favorite song now," he said. "It's from *The Music Man*. Do you want to hear some of the words?"

I did.

Looking closely at me he sang in a soft but clear voice: "There were birds all around / But I never heard them singing, / No, I never heard them at all / Till there was you."

Some thirty years afterward I made good on a promise I had made to Josh's mother, to write her son's story. I located my former client and pupil and took him a copy of the book, which I had titled *Fill Me Up to Empty*. I learned that the theater continued to play an important role in his life. Josh told me about his roles in community theatrical productions and about receiving recognition for his performance in a recent show. We had dinner together and talked about books and art and music. I remembered how well the theater and music had served Josh when he was a child, not just in his aspirations as a performer but as something that gave deep meaning to his life.

Josh now lives in a community home and holds down a responsible job in a retail chain for children, where he is responsible for keeping the shelves of books, toys, and musical items stocked. He is active in his church, has learned to sail, volunteers in community theater, and reads from a wide selection of books. My visit with him was profound. I was flooded with memories of his incredibly difficult childhood struggle to understand his chaotic life and to make a place for himself in a world that for him was both frightening and undecipherable. We talked about his gains and the struggles he still faces. He was neither bitter nor angry. Instead, there was a calm serenity about him. Seeing how far he had come brought tears to my eyes.

Creativity is one of the strongest connections we have to life. It is one of the most powerful forms of expressing our right to be. Creativity can be defined in as many ways as it can be conceived. I see it as a spiritual energy that nurtures our vitality—a powerful way to celebrate who we are. Creative energy is all around us, whether we are singing a song, writing a masterpiece, or folding laundry. Every original act asserts our commitment to life. When we create, we plant ourselves firmly in the moment and teach ourselves that what we do matters.

Josh is a reminder that we do not "find" happiness at work—we take it with us. If we say yes to the creativity within us, then it can be a free channel from the eternal source into the world, lifting our spirits and enriching our work lives.

40

Stress in the Workplace

"WHEN I WAS A KID I WANTED TO BE A HERMIT," my client Jess said. "I thought that teaching would be a compromise because I was good with young people, and I thought I could close the classroom door, shut out the rest of the world, and do my thing. Seems I forgot about little things like a demanding principal, angry parents, and state regulations."

Jess had come to talk about job stress and her need to make some changes. She decided to go back to school and get her master's degree in marine biology. She then tried working with a water management group. She thought she could be alone outside in jeans and boots, preserving natural resources. After three years in the marshes and swamps of Florida, Jess quit that job, returned home, and resumed counseling. "I got tired of swatting mosquitoes and watching my decisions be overturned because of politics," she explained.

Next, Jess took a job with a state regulatory agency in resource management in another state. This time her stress came from being in a position to approve or deny permits, and from the unpleasant discovery of the political issues involved at times in the decision making.

"What do you think is the uniting theme in these jobs?" I asked her.

"Much of my stress comes from all of the responsibility and none of the authority. I can't look the other way when I see something going on that I believe is just plain wrong."

No one gets a pass on stress. It is a fact of life, and we need to know that nothing is wrong with us when we experience it. Accepting its inevitability frees up time and energy for developing strategies to deal with it.

Stress is normal and motivates us to meet challenges. But when stress occurs to an extent the human body cannot handle, physical, psychosocial, and behavioral problems can occur. Whether stress arises from the workplace or our personal lives, *our cells do not know the difference*. Cells do not distinguish between a bullet and a baseball, between "good" and "bad" stressors, such as losing a job or being offered a promotion. High levels of stress accumulated over time can lead to a breakdown in our functioning. If we react to stress by abusing drugs or using alcohol to become comfortably numb, we only add to the damage.

Stress begins in childhood, especially stress related to achievement. I once worked with a woman from a high-achieving family in which every member had an advanced degree in medicine or law. Although she held a master's degree and was a hospital administrator, when she was passed over for a promotion she became depressed.

"I feel as though I have wasted my life, that my career has meant nothing," she said. Her self-esteem, largely tied up in her career, hit rock bottom. This is a familiar story about stress in the workplace. When self-esteem is linked almost exclusively to the job we do, we are out of balance. If we don't keep a healthy balance between work and play, between tension and happy lightheartedness, we break down. Think of the body as a big battery. If we don't recharge it, we run out of energy. We get sick, irritable, depressed, unreasonable, and anxious.

What can we do to balance stress? Nature provides outlets such as sleep, rest, healthy foods, exercise, laughter, play. Sometimes we denigrate natural things and let the marketplace tell us what will ease our stress—membership in a swanky club, a BMW, twelve-year-old scotch. We don't always give reverence to the natural things that serve us. Simple things truly do help reduce stress. Laughter is one of the easiest and best ways to lower stress. Also, learning to breathe with deep, slow breaths and doing stretching exercises are activities simple enough to do almost anywhere, and they take only a few seconds.

I find that people handle stress in the workplace as well or as poorly as they handle it in other areas of life. I recommend daily awareness of how well we're doing. We can check our stress meter every morning when we wake up. Do we get a "happy" energy reading or is the meter showing dread, resentment, lack of enthusiasm, lack of enjoyment? If the latter, the annual vacation or the monthly massage won't take care of things. Stress management is a matter of daily balance.

In looking at strategies for managing stress, we need to recognize and accept the stressors in our lives. Once we take a realistic look at what our stressors are, we can then begin to prioritize, say no to certain things, and exercise our freedom to make choices that are in our own best interest. In many cases, *we need to face the relative unimportance of our role in the workplace* and take better advantage of the freedom we have for change.

Jess called me recently and came in for a consultation. "The hermit is restless again," she said. She had made a move in her organization that had eased the situation for three years, but she continued to experience high-level stress involved in implementing rules and regulations. "I'm ready to find a way to be my own boss and manage myself. I'm tired of running scared about doing what will make me happy."

Accepting responsibility for the quality of our days allows us to stop blaming others for our lot in life. Not everyone has the choices open to them that Jess has. But we often have more freedom than we think. It is difficult, but not impossible, to take responsibility for each day, one at a time. And don't fight Mother Nature. This means rest when you are weary, drink water when you are thirsty, laugh and play when you are burdened with work. Identify what makes you feel good and is good for you, and try to do it regularly (dancing, watching movies, walking your dog, hanging out with friends). Love is a great antidote for stress. Don't forget to use your support system of family and friends. If all this is not enough, seek out a professional who can help you learn to manage workplace stress and to divert some of your energy to activities which bring you pure pleasure. Remember: the purpose of life is to be joyous and free. What can you do today to fulfill your destiny?

41

Why Can't You Just Listen to Me?

WHEN I WAS A KID I *NEVER* HEARD ANYONE SAY, "When I grow up I want to be a listener!" I never heard a school guidance counselor encourage *anyone* to consider a career in listening. I wondered why, since there is such a demand for good listeners. The market is wide open. Positions go unfilled. Demand always exceeds supply.

I think the demand is there because one of our most basic human needs is to understand and to be understood. So I knew very early that my life's work would involve being a good listener. It is a skill of value in any workplace where there is more than one pair of ears.

Over the decades, I have seen the profound benefits that occur as part of the listening process. I have experienced some of my most profitable professional moments as a psychologist, sometimes as the listener and sometimes as the person being listened to.

Listening with detachment accelerates growth. Such listening comes from a connection with what I call impersonal love—love of life, love of self, a commitment to happiness, especially in the work world that consumes so many years of our lives. My wish is that whatever your career choice, you will experience genuine communication. In that spirit I offer some of my observations for would-be good listeners.

Have you ever witnessed a scene like this: around the office water cooler someone says, "Sorry you didn't get that promotion you expected. But you're lucky! My uncle Joe got laid off, and he has three children." What's this response really saying? "Your problem is not important. *You* are not important—my story can trump yours." To be a good listener, you have to keep the focus on the other person. For the moment, it's all about them.

In our nervousness, we often rush to find a quick solution and start giving advice. You don't *have* to solve the problem before the discussion ends. When we rush, it's often an indication of *our* anxiousness or discomfort, not of the other person's needs.

Be careful not to tell people what they should or shouldn't do or feel. Let them express themselves. Ask questions and then sit back while solutions do or do not present themselves. Your job is to accept and respect the feelings—to be the witness, not the judge.

Think of listening as your attempt to *share the load.* In my work I have listened to mothers describe the loss of a child to rape, suicide, addictions, or automobile wrecks. Some tell me it is the first time they have ever fully shared their story. It is a powerful experience to witness the healing that follows the telling. Happiness begins with being listened to and understood. And happiness is contagious.

Don't presume to know what is needed from you. Instead, ask "How can I be of help?" "What do you need?" The ball is in their court—where it belongs.

If their story seems truly serious and relevant to the job at hand, ask what kind of remedy is available. If you both feel out of your league, ask for permission to share the information with someone with the authority to help. Then seek someone out who can aid in solving the problem.

One of the reasons that demand for listeners exceeds supply is that it isn't easy being a good listener. You must begin, as always, with listening to *your* needs; you must take care of *yourself* in this process. Problems won't always come at convenient times. Sometimes you have to say, "Can I call you back? I'm just walking out the door for an appointment." To be a good listener, you must remember to make the call.

Look at listening experiences as an opportunity to improve your valuable marketing skills, to expand *your* own self-awareness and self-control, to enrich *your* life. Reflect on the process. If listening were always easy, we would not hear the words so commonly screamed in homes across America every night, "Why can't you just listen to me?"

Finally, what do you do when you are forced to hear the thing you most fear? The boss delivers the news: "You're fired." Or your spouse says: "I don't love you anymore." Or your teenager says: "I'm in trouble." If you appreciate the value of being a good listener, you will listen silently, holding the flames of rage, fear, and pain inside until you are in safe company—the company of a good listener.

42

The Power of the Unseen

I'LL BE THE MOMMY, YOU BE THE BABY. . . . *I'm a choo-choo train. . . . I'm the teacher, listen to me. . . . Let's pretend that we're going to the moon.* To many of us, this is what childhood is about: the ability to be anything we want to be. Creative, make-believe play allows children to act out their wishes and fears. It promotes cognitive development and helps children learn to communicate, to share, and to develop empathy for others. There is something inborn in us that requires this outlet. Indeed, there is a huge industry made up of those who give their entire life to creating imaginary characters for movies, plays, music, and games.

Imagination is an important and humanizing quality. There is a strong correlation between imagination, creativity, and happiness. Imagination and creativity allow us access to our unconscious. Every exercise in imagination contains some profound meaning. It is one of the gifts nature gives us to help us discover who we are; it is how we envision a future. Literally and figuratively, once we imagine something, it becomes a possibility.

A friend, now a retired college teacher, still remembers vividly her imaginary play as a young child: "At my School for Stuffed Animals, attendance was never a problem. My soft, cuddly students sat in their assigned seats and did what I asked them to do. There was never any rebellion, never a cross word. My helper was my doll, Suzanna. Once class began, I would tear up little scraps of paper to hand out, along with stubby pencils, for my pupils to write assignments on. I would later collect the papers, grade them, and hand them back." As a child, my friend did not know the meaning of her play. It was soon clear to the adults around her that she had it in her to become a gifted teacher. For her, the elaborate game brought out the content of the unconscious, which then became real.

Parents tend to encourage imagination in young children, but in adolescents often fear the imagination and try to extinguish it. The problem with setting limits too tightly is that the adolescent's imagination is not extinguished, but goes underground, and can show up in hostile, even dangerous behaviors. Better to show interest in whatever captures your child's fancy, learn about it, and discuss your feelings about it openly, honestly and clearly. Then stand close by as your child makes decisions and experiences consequences—even ones you hate like, say, a tattoo of a skull. Your son or daughter is learning that not everything that can be imagined should be done.

Imagination without discernment can be as dangerous as when cells in our body go awry and produce cancer. It is also a problem when too much emphasis on imagination creates emotional disturbances. Imagination only—without concrete manifestation—becomes a flight from life. Imagination without practical application is like a television screen with no picture, or a theater with no play to perform. The unseen power is unrealized and untested. How can we know the value of our imaginings unless we check them out with others in the real world?

The more self-awareness we have as adults, the better we understand the literal meaning of what is in the imagination. We have learned the great joy of turning an imagined architectural plan, musical concept, or dream vacation into reality. With judgment, experience, *and* our fantasies, life is good!

However, everyone occasionally experiences the great unseen powers without thinking about it. It may be a power that builds or destroys. We need to be careful what we turn our mind to, because our feet will follow. Whatever our mindset, we will find confirmation of our belief in the world around us. Thought is energy. The important thing is understanding that our thoughts color—some say "create"—our lives in concrete ways.

An example of one way this unseen power affects us can be seen in everyday misunderstandings between loved ones. A friend told me that when her father-in-law was approaching death from painful cancer, people who came to see him were abusing him, crying and telling him their problems. She wanted to put a stop to these visits and protect this man she loved. Her father-in-law's reaction was quite different. "It has just come to me that my whole life is a prayer," he told his daughter-in-law. Then he asked her not to turn people away. "My ministry now is to let them come and stretch their souls." He saw his death as an opportunity. Her imagined scenario, colored by her unconscious beliefs, was that he needed to be protected. Open conversation resolved the conflicting realities.

It is not about right or wrong, important or unimportant, but rather about a fundamental truth: the unseen has power that will enrich our lives if we pay attention to it and maintain a healthy respect for imagination and its concrete consequences. Whether it is an imaginary playmate, a role played in the theater, a dream, or a vision that propels us into action, our imagination allows us to tap into the awesome energy of the unconscious. The power is the unconscious *behind* the imagination. That is one way we get to ultimate truths.

43

Take a Break

"HOW BEAUTIFUL IT IS TO DO NOTHING, and then rest afterward," the magnet on my refrigerator reminds me daily. It's a profound message that I have delivered to hundreds of clients over the years. So many people do not know how to rest and relax. Instead, they are on the go all the time. Overdoing seems to be our illness. Regardless of the cause, the symptom for many is the inability to rest the body and quiet the mind.

This is a serious problem because rest and relaxation are critical to maintaining a high energy level, a positive outlook, and a healthy immune system. Without sufficient rest, we have difficulty concentrating and remembering. We become grumpy, impatient, and no fun to be around.

"My mind and my body are always in high gear," my client Connie said. "It's affecting my health."

"Sounds like you feel driven," I said.

"I feel like a runaway train."

"And what drives this train?" I asked.

"Worry, fear, and guilt. I worry if I'm not totally busy, totally stressed, always at full throttle."

"What are you afraid of?"

"That I'm not good enough, that I haven't justified my existence, that I'm a useless lump."

"And the guilt?"

"Oh, that comes easy," Connie said. "I'm embarrassed that I have so much money. There's something in there about not deserving the good things that happen to me."

"So you think if you stay so busy, you can keep those feelings at bay?"

"Yes, but it doesn't work!" Connie screeched.

"Maybe it's not so much what you're doing, as what you're *not* doing," I said.

As we explored each negative emotion, Connie began to limit her activities, to spend time each day in quiet relaxation. Instead of racing through six activities before breakfast, she began to lie quietly in bed for a few minutes before getting up. She started an herb garden and hung bird feeders. She read books that had been on her "to-do list" for years. She learned yoga and meditation. "And my friends like the change they see," she reported months later.

"You know when you said to me, 'Don't just *do* something; *stand* there?' Well, I finally got it," Connie said. "It's not about what I do; it's about who I am. Most days now, I can identify what is driving my need to do everything, be everything, fix everything. The train no longer feels out of control. There's a new engineer at the throttle."

For Connie, overdoing came from a negative belief system. Changing her beliefs about herself helped her slow down, to enjoy life, and to achieve more. Negative attitudes and low self-esteem can cause us to overcompensate and overdo. Another cause stems from the inherent stressors of life, which have a physical impact on our bodies.

One of my physician friends explained: "Working under pressure or stress all the time pumps the adrenaline. High adrenaline levels make us feel restless and overstimulated. If you can step back and let go, there's a chance of lowering the adrenaline level." My friend goes on to advise that, at work, we take a lunch break—let everything go; walk away for a while. "You'll find your efficiency improves," she adds. Her comments are echoed in the *Tao Te Ching,* the "Way" of the ancient Chinese wisdom literature of Taoism: "Do your work, then step back. The only path to serenity."

Walter Russell believed that by focusing on a discipline for no more than two hours at a time, he could optimize his performance. Russell therefore sometimes worked two hours a day on each of five activities. He became a noted musician, a book illustrator and author, a portrait painter, and a highly renowned architect who built world-famous public buildings. At age fifty-six, Russell turned his interests to sculpture. His subjects included Thomas Edison and Franklin Roosevelt, Charles Goodyear, and General Douglas MacArthur.

Russell used physical rest to draw on his creative, intuitive side, and he rested his mind with competitive sports, becoming a well-known equestrian and ice skater. How could he do all this? Because of "my knowledge of my unity with the Universal One," he said. In other words, for Russell, physical activity constituted a vacation from more quiet, creative, physically static endeavors. His belief served him well throughout his life.

We do not need to spend two hours each on five different things a day. What we decide to do with the energy we have depends on our age and situation. The issue is misapplied energy—overdoing, as opposed to focused, applied energy. Connie's misdirected energy, driven by worry, fear, and guilt, resulted in physical exhaustion and discontent. Misapplied energy is a waste. Steam is not worth anything if it is not harnessed. Russell is an example of someone aware of, and in harmony with, the universal source of energy. He is in Tao. Learning how to apply this free-flowing energy, and knowing where it comes from, allows us to balance rest and work. Rest is necessary for replenishment, and if we rest and relax, the energy needed will follow. "Practice not-doing, and everything will fall into place," reads the *Tao Te Ching*.

Now that you've finished reading this chapter, before you get busy with your next task, sit for a few moments and quiet your mind. Don't *do* anything. Just rest.

lesson seven

The Knack of Happy Parenting

Children
Can easily open the
Drawer

That lets the spirit rise up and wear
Its favorite costume of
Mirth and laughter.

—HAFIZ

The knack of enjoying children is to be interested in them—to pay attention and to learn along with them. We do have a responsibility to care for our children, but we also have the opportunity to learn from them. If we pay attention to each child, we see that he or she is not a blank slate upon which we get to write whatever we want. If we develop a genuine relationship with them, we see each child as a fascinating combination of traits and temperaments.

The wise parent works with the bent of the child rather than going against it. When your child mirrors something you don't like, take a moment to ask yourself: "Where does this come from?" When my son was four, he walked around the house for days saying "ohdamen" in a singsong voice. With each utterance, he would emphasize a different syllable of the mysterious sound. I had no idea what this word was or meant, and it was driving me crazy.

"When he grows up, I hope he remembers this and can tell us what it meant," I said to his father. Finally, I had the bright idea of simply asking my son: "Who says 'Ohdamen'?" I asked.

"You do," he said.

I was startled. "When?" I asked.

"When you spilled the sprinkles. When you made the cupcakes for our party," he answered.

Of course! I had been rushing to decorate cupcakes before my son's birthday party. I spilled an entire box of decorative sugar sprinkles and watched them roll over the kitchen floor, under the table, chairs, refrigerator, stove. "Oh, damn it!" I had muttered, not knowing that my son heard me. Now knowing what he was trying to say, I made a quick recovery.

"That's right," I said. "But we say that word only when we spill the sprinkles."

"Well, okay," my son said. "But can we have some cupcakes?"

The knack of being a happy parent begins with curiosity and ends in delight. Wake up each day and borrow wisdom from the Christian tradition, the words Jesus heard from his heavenly father: "This is my beloved child in whom I am well pleased," and then look for ways to be pleased all day long. Think of the first Christmas. Baby Jesus just showed up to be adored. I believe that's my job as a parent—to adore my child.

The stories you will read in this chapter allow reflection on the role of parenting and especially on what child psychiatrist D. W.

Winnicott many years ago described as "good-enough parenting." None of the people whose stories appear here had perfect, loving, caring parents. No parent can have everything, know everything, be everything a child needs. But we all have what it takes to learn the knack of "good-enough parenting." What's essential in this process is eternal. In difficult situations, go back to eternal truths. And since there are very few eternal truths, it makes life as a parent simpler!

44

Keeping Cool with Your Kids

WHAT HELPS KEEP PSYCHOLOGISTS LIKE ME in business are children and adolescents whose risky behaviors scare parents silly. Parents fear for their child's safety in a dangerous world, yet they know that their youngster will—and should—take risks. Frantic, concerned parents seek help for, and understanding of, children who are fighting, failing in school, getting suspended, being arrested, or selecting friends who may lead them down a terrifying path towards substance abuse, pregnancy, or reckless, destructive, heart-stopping foolishness.

"This is not the child I used to know," parents say. "How did we come to this place? What can I do? How can I make my child shape up?" As mothers and fathers, we know we are in big trouble when we see our children floundering. We wish we could risk-proof them, but we know that we can't. Even so, while we cannot *protect* our children from all harm, we can *prepare* them for the risks they will take.

To do this, we must understand and transcend the tension of opposites. Imagine parents trying to handle two hot potatoes. In one hand is fear—fear of life-threatening dangers such as car wrecks, drug dealers, kidnappers, rapists. It is the fear of not having control, while at the same time knowing deep down that this kind of control is impossible. Besides the fear of the outside world, there is the fear of self, of our own inability as parents to manage situations, causing many of us to make knee-jerk decisions that only worsen matters, actions to decrease our own anxiety and fear.

The other hot potato is the wish to rear the perfect child—the smartest, the cutest, the first to walk—the vindication of all our own failures and disappointments. Parents juggling this particular hot potato seek to remove risk by making every decision for their child. They do not want their children to experience pain and stress, to face failure and challenges. Their goal is to protect them from hurtful experiences.

This, in fact, is the impossible dream depicted in the story of Siddhartha, the prince who would become a Buddha. His father, the king, set out to shield the prince from all the stresses and suffering of life. Because he was a very powerful king, he was able to succeed for many years. What a great source of wisdom the world would have missed had he been completely successful. Luckily, Siddhartha learned to transcend, rather than to avoid, suffering.

Our goal as parents should not be to remove risks, even if we could. Risking the unknown is one of the most important things we ever do, and preparing our children for the risks they will take is one of the greatest gifts we can give them. Our quest as parents is to transcend these two extremes, being everything or being nothing—the rule-bound, overly strict controller or the absentee parent abdicating responsibility and blaming outside influences, unwilling to look inward.

Transcending means parents can allow a new reality to freely emerge, one that is organic and true. To do so requires an understanding of this natural process—to hold on to what we *know* is true and to examine what we *think* we know and what we *think* is true. Our children's development often depends upon our own continued growth.

Parents are co-evolutionary forces with nature in that through parenting they can participate in the selection process, helping children decide from the vast array of choices put before them. Danger comes when children lack what they need to optimize their potential. Parents can be soul-affirming to their children by communicating over and over again that ancient message: "You are my beloved child, in whom I am well pleased."

By seeking wisdom, offering opportunities for learning and reflecting *with* their children, parents can transcend fear and model what their children need. As parents we provide living examples of ways we have navigated key transitions our children also will face.

But what happens when parents have not had good role models themselves? In this case, we still can learn to parent well, but it helps if we can follow another's example. I was an adult when I took my first swimming lesson. My parents did not swim, so I had no model to go by. But I developed a picture in my mind by watching a swimming master glide gracefully through the water. I was able to take heart that my floundering efforts would pay off.

When parenting, we can turn to wise friends, other parents with different skills, and experienced teachers and counselors. Parents need a community of support that is encouraging, innovative, instructive, flexible, and inspirational, and they need a liberal sprinkling of humor and lightheartedness, too.

When scary, painful information about our children comes our way, perspective is an important key to maintaining our sanity. As one college freshman wrote:

> Dear Mom and Dad,
>
> I'm sorry I haven't been in touch, but I had to move into another dorm when my room burned. I was in the infirmary for a week and then had to borrow clothes to get to class since

> all mine burned. But don't worry, my burns are healing nicely and I won't need much plastic surgery. Actually, none of this really happened. But I DID flunk physics, and I wanted you to receive this information in its proper perspective.
>
> Love, Joe.

Joe's letter to his parents reminds us that our children need our unconditional love. Giving that love is a tall order that requires us to reach deep into ourselves, to know our strengths and weaknesses, to hold on to a belief system that sustains us when the going gets rough and to have a support system which nourishes us.

45

Happy Non-Hyper Holidays

AHHH . . . THE HOLIDAY SEASON. Chestnuts roasting on an open fire. There's no place like home for the holidays. Silent night.... Happiness, peace, joy, and family togetherness is the goal. But the holidays become stressful for all of us if we aren't careful, and even more so if we have children who get hyped up with days filled with events which leave them—and us—overwhelmed and exhausted.

Most of what I have learned about happy—not hyper—holidays is pretty simple. But our materialistic culture, with its advertising-driven push, is always with us. We may have to consciously work against this process, which can be distracting and upsetting. In our role as parents of young or adult children, there are things we can do to raise our level of joy and minimize our level of stress.

When my clients have trouble with children's behavior, I find one of the first and most effective things they can do during the holiday season is to turn off the TV. Television exists to sell products. It is an organ for advertising. It holds our attention by constant hype. Children are less likely to want what they haven't seen! This one act would transform the holiday season. One of our great writers and social observers, Norman Mailer, was asked what *one* thing could be done to change America for the better. He made the bold statement that *the best thing* we could do for our children would be to ban advertising from television.

Without the distraction of television, families can play games, read, talk to each other, plan to take a meal to a needy family during the holidays, buy a gift for a needy child. "Over the river and through the woods" nostalgia is a natural human longing, but we need to spend less time on trying to recreate the past and instead face life as it really is and make the very best we can of it. Most of our children have never seen chestnuts roasting over an open fire and most likely have never arrived at Grandma's in a horse-drawn sleigh. And it is a real miracle if harried parents can find a "silent night" in which "all is calm" for themselves during the holiday season.

At Thanksgiving, one way to keep the family focused on the meaning of the day is to verbalize whatever we are grateful for. Be ready by keeping a gratitude list all year round. I like the sign I saw on a church bulletin board recently, which said, "Want to get rich quick? Count your blessings!" In teaching our children about unselfishness, we need to speak our sense of gratitude out loud, telling them each day at least one thing we are grateful for. Little by little, it will make a difference to them.

The high energy of the holiday season can cause children to be disruptive, distracted, overstimulated, and unhappy. This can be especially true of children with special needs. To prevent distraction from turning into annoyance and anger, build in routines for those who do not handle sudden changes well. We need to verbalize for even very young children what is to come. "After your nap, we are going to get in the car and drive to Grandma's house." Later, before leaving, you can say, "In five minutes we will get in the car and go see Grandma." As you walk toward the door, it helps to say again, "Now we're going to Grandma's house."

All kids benefit from practicing for new experiences. Much of the stress of holidays occurs when parents have certain expectations for their children's performance at family or social gatherings, but fail to notify their children. Preparing children ahead of time and respecting the whole family's needs goes a long way in averting get-together disasters. Once you've done this, be consistent. Don't stir the pot with last-minute changes.

Perhaps most important to remember during the holidays is that each child has his or her own needs, and it is incumbent upon us not to assume that their needs are the same as ours. If we listen closely to the questions they ask, we can allay some of their anxieties.

As his family prepared to have Thanksgiving dinner with his grandparents, six-year-old Toby asked his mother the same questions two years in a row: "Is Grandma still going to pinch my cheeks when she hugs me? Can I sit at the grown-ups' table? Do I have to clean my plate? Can I have more than one dessert? Are we spending the night there?"

Instead of screaming, "Shut up! Can't you see I'm busy?" take one quiet moment to listen to what lies behind the question. The child is nervous about going and may need a greater sense of control over how he or she is treated. Thoughtful responses can help a child feel better prepared for a holiday celebration: "Your grandmother doesn't know how you feel about having your cheeks pinched, so you could tell her. And you could ask her how old kids have to be to sit at the grown-ups' table. Then maybe you'll be more comfortable spending the night." You will be amply rewarded by your child's more appropriate behavior.

It is critical that amid the hustle and bustle, we create quiet time for our children and for ourselves. Children pick up the tab for how parents are handling the holiday season. We are the ones who teach our children what the holidays are about. If we want them to take time to think, to reflect, to rest, we need to make that same kind of time for ourselves. Before we admonish our children to "settle down" we can remind *ourselves* to settle down. We can prioritize our to-do list, do the most important things first and forget the rest. We can make time for quiet thoughts. How? Get up fifteen minutes early, sit in a quiet, comfortable place and don't *do* anything—just *be*. It makes a difference.

If you prepare ahead, if you set realistic goals, and stick as closely to your regular routine as possible, you can find ways not only to maintain your sanity and your family's during the holidays, but to actually enjoy each occasion and get in touch with its true meaning. It is not easy to find time for ourselves when we feel pulled in so many different directions. But if we do, we discover that the payoff is enormous, not just for ourselves but for our families.

Finally, it helps if you're not trying to do this alone. Involve others in your effort. Then accept that this holiday doesn't have to be "the best ever." It rarely is, and anyway, how would we know until a few years have passed? Don't let unrealistic expectations weigh you down and prevent you from finding your own meaning in holiday traditions and celebrations.

46

Can't Buy Love

"MY SON, CHARLIE, ONLY SEVEN AT THE TIME, pushed a shopping cart down the toy aisle at Christmas," my friend said. "He grabbed boxes, first from the left aisle and then from the right, tossing them in the cart and saying with a big smile, 'Here, this will be good for somebody; somebody will like to play with this.' He had no idea what he was selecting and who would be the recipients."

Twenty years later, his mother is still doing the same thing! "I always wait until the last minute, and then I toss items in the cart, sounding just like my son: This will be good for *somebody*."

Why do we find ourselves in long lines buying things with little thought, just to check that name off our list? Why do we spend too much on gifts for weddings, Christmas, and birthdays? Why do we buy over-the-top presents for children? We do it for the same reasons we identify with our new car or take pride in our cool new cell phone. We have in our culture a confusion of values, a misperception of where happiness comes from. We believe that we *are* what we own; that human beings are as worthwhile as the things they possess.

"You're only as valuable as what someone will pay you," my client's angry husband said when she announced that she was going back to college to major in literature. "Nobody is going to pay you for being able to quote some obscure poet. It's a total waste."

There are gifts that bring us pleasure and meet our needs. And there are gifts that are touching and special, even though not what we asked for. It has little to do with being rich or poor. The first year of my marriage, my husband learned that I loved Mahalia Jackson and I wanted her latest LP record. On Christmas morning, I opened my special gift from him, wrapped neatly and tied with a red ribbon. I was disappointed to find inside not one but *six* record albums—of Ella Fitzgerald!

My good friend responded to her parents' request to tell them what she most wanted for the holidays. She didn't hesitate. "Paul Simon's *Graceland* CD," she said. When it came time to open presents, she tore into her parents' gift first. It was extremely difficult, she recalled, for her to get excited about the two beige hand towels she found under the red and white tissue paper.

Sometimes when we *do* get what we ask for, it doesn't make us happy. Bonnie desperately wanted a pair of blue suede shoes of a particular brand so she would fit in as a freshman in high school. Her grandmother at first refused to buy the shoes that cost $150, pointing out that her granddaughter needed more practical things. "But, Grandmother, I don't want anything else. This present will make me so happy." The shoes were purchased and Bonnie and her grandmother got in the car. Before they left the parking lot, Bonnie began to cry. "I thought these shoes would make me feel better," she sobbed. "But they don't. Now I feel even worse." Her grandmother never saw Bonnie wear the shoes.

As parents we need to acknowledge that some of our gifts carry a heavy burden of expectations. We want elaborate thank-yous, a happy face, eternal gratitude. One severely depressed teen described her absent father's birthday present this way: "Here are the strings; no gift attached."

We also need to accept that the presents we buy our children may not address their desires. Desire is never completely satisfied. So whatever we give, we must give from a full heart, not from a place of guilt or pressure, or in the mistaken notion that our gifts are "making up" for something. And we don't need to sit waiting for rivers of thanks and appreciation to flow from those we've just swamped with "things" they had convinced us they couldn't do without.

What would parents have to *give up* if they decided to rethink and redefine their gift-giving? First of all, parents of young children would have to give up that time-honored threat heard everywhere for weeks before Christmas: "If you aren't good, Santa isn't coming to see you!" The silence in many households and public places would be deafening! Parents would have to give up the belief that they can buy their children a better childhood; give up the fear of losing their children's love and the fear of their children's anger and disappointment. They would have to give up their fear of being criticized by people important to them. And they would have to look at their fear that their youngsters don't have the strength to stand up to other children's comments, or the ability to understand and accept a different way of looking at gifts—from the point of view of a giver as well as a receiver.

Not giving children an opportunity to balance receiving gifts with giving gifts is a vote of "no confidence" in their innate goodness and ability to learn about compassionate giving. If it all feels too overwhelming, start small. Talk to your family about the needs of others. Identify people in need in your community and elsewhere in the world and find out how to share.

Likewise, make a change in your gift-giving to your adult family and friends. Give gifts to charities in their names. Encourage your children to give of themselves to a worthwhile project and see it through. Expose them to people who make it a vital part of their lives to give to those truly in need. Model an attitude of balance between giving and receiving. This change in attitude is difficult and does not happen overnight. But it is a worthy goal. It leads children to lives of peace and happiness.

47

In Praise of Committed Fathers

FELIX CHE PUC IS THE FATHER OF FOUR DAUGHTERS and grandfather of three granddaughters. Over the years I have come to know him and his family intimately because, despite my so-called Western sophistication, I have needed him. He was born in a small village in Mexico near Chichen Itza, among the remnants of the Mayan civilization. He grew up speaking Mayan and inherited the Mayan culture of his ancestors.

Felix moved to Isla Mujeres when he was a teenager. In his rich life he has been a farmer, a matador, a fisherman, a taxi driver, a builder, and a property manager. Full of humor, always at your service, seeing nothing as too demeaning or too difficult, he makes things happen all over Isla for occasional guests like me, for his friends, and most of all for his family. For Felix, there is little separation between work life and family life.

During the many years that I have known him as I visit the island, Felix has taught me much about what it is to be a human being in the highest sense. But perhaps what I admire most about Felix is what a great father he is. So I celebrate him, and through his story, all the committed fathers who every day strive to be good role models for their children.

"What is it like to be the father of four daughters?" I asked Felix.

He smiled. "Each of my daughters has her own character, and God gave each one her own gifts. My oldest daughter, Alejandra, has the gift of love and takes care of people. She did not go to the university. She married and is a wonderful mother. The whole family can depend on her. She's given my wife Elizabeth and me three granddaughters who are growing as they should. She makes us very proud.

"My second daughter, Merley, is a scholar. She's read many books, and she brings this knowledge to our family. She had cancer when she was younger, and the whole village made it possible for her to get the treatment she needed. Then I sold our house to have money to send her to college. She's tops in her classes now. A documentary she made recently won a big award.

"My third daughter, Soledad, is the practical one. She works hard at school and she's making it easier for Elizabeth and me to send her to college. Soledad has a special gift for math and wants to become an engineer.

"My youngest daughter, Ruth, is popular and has many friends. She is gifted in music and wins awards for her singing. She wants to play guitar and perform. My job is to help her slow down and to do her school work.

"Each child is different," said Felix. "Elizabeth and I see our job as understanding and supporting them."

From my own professional experience, what seems simple and obvious to Felix is rare and quite profound. He knows who he is and how important his parenting is, and he knows how to support his daughters as individuals. In our society, we undervalue and overlook the importance of fathers' parenting.

When it comes to daughters, clearly their father is the first man in their lives. Fathers play a unique and potent role in developing the self-image of young women. The father of a young daughter has the opportunity to set the standard of what it means to be in relationship with a man. When young women are bombarded with outrageous media messages about the importance of how they look, a father can hold up a different mirror for his daughter to peer into. He can tell her that these messages are wrong; that he values who she is, what she has to say, her spunk, her soul. From my experience, I believe that how a young woman perceives herself as a friend, lover, wife, mother, and colleague is to a large extent influenced by the love and acceptance she experienced with her father or father surrogate in her earlier years.

Research shows that fathers' healthy relationships with their sons helps prevent psychological maladjustments such as substance abuse, depression, and behavioral problems. Young men who maintain a close, loving, supportive relationship with their father are much less likely to experience low self-esteem, to become depressed and suicidal, or to drop out of school. If fathers believed this and accepted this awesome responsibility, our young people would live healthier and more meaningful lives.

Several years ago, I was called in early January to see Jason, a high school junior who was contemplating suicide after the Christmas holidays. His parents had been divorced for many years, and the only time he heard from his father was during the holiday season when his father would ask his son what he wanted for Christmas. Jason would mention something, and his father would send it to him. This Christmas he had told his father what he wanted—a larger, more expensive gift. The holidays passed and the gift never arrived. Depressed and suicidal, Jason took his father off the hook. "I guess this year I just asked for too much," he said listlessly.

As I think about Felix, I also remember the many lost, floundering, fatherless young people like Jason I have known and worked with. No amount of praise is too much for the dedicated fathers—the unsung heroes—who *do* show up and make a difference in their children's lives.

48

The Good-Enough Parent

PARENTS WHO CAN EXPRESS THEIR LOVE for their children in ways their children can feel and believe in allow them to take risks into the unknown that are growth-producing and soul-making. Without certainty of their parents' love, children are likely to take risks leading to self-loathing and self-destruction.

As parents we quickly find out how easy it is to have the limits of our love and acceptance tested. The list of our trials and tribulations is endless. Our children regularly test our capacity for love by their bad choice of peers, their tattoos or body piercings, their lackluster academic performance, their insistence on dating or marrying a loser, their dream of becoming a rock star or some other impossible career choice, their experimentation with or addiction to drugs or alcohol. Then there are problems not of their choosing: handicaps, illnesses, pregnancies, the relationship with the "other" parent in separation and divorce, being gay—the minefields for parents and children are ever present.

We've been told that it takes an entire village to rear a child. Rearing children in isolation, away from family, without a "village" for support is too much for parents. Children reared in such a spare atmosphere often miss out on the nurturance, encouragement, support, and affirmation they will need when later they face choices and make decisions that will be self-destructive or growth producing.

To many parents, the idea of being a significant part of a village is alien. Many parents live far away from their families; many single parents who are forced to work long hours to provide for their children feel there is little time to pursue village connections. As a society we Americans don't make it easy. We have always been stratified socioeconomically, but now we are stratified geographically and by age. Most children no longer live among grandparents and great-grandparents; no wonder they no longer value the wisdom and insights their elders have to offer. In too many day care centers, children are raising our children, working for minimum wage. Retirement communities that might benefit the elderly rob us of the experience of caring for elderly relatives. Having no role models for this kind of selfless caregiving, we are ill-equipped to provide quality care and love and support to the opposite end of the spectrum—to small children. We as parents can falter in this awesome task, in part because we have not benefited from an apprenticeship with master teachers who can model unconditional love toward us.

Literally going back to village life is impossible, but we can build for ourselves a healthy support system and then make constructive use of it. This is an important coping skill, which we often forget when we are under stress or feeling overwhelmed. Mothers and fathers need a community of people to count on for support in parenting. Parents need others to speak with openly, people we can count on to support us as a parent. Having a number of people in your village that you can depend on is important for your emotional health, and therefore also for the emotional well-being of your child. Parents with a good support system tend to be less depressed and anxious and more optimistic than those with a weak support system. And those parents who feel a part of a village are more successful at overcoming depression and feelings of loneliness. Listen to Clara's story:

"For me to become a decent parent, I needed help. The job was too unrelenting, too demanding, too depleting of energy, too mysterious for a mother alone—especially a young, immature, lonely, depressed, confused, angry mother. I know. I was that mother. Isolated in a new town chosen by my husband's career goals, lonely in a big house in need of furnishings and repair, immature, though an educated young professional, I was completely drained by caring for a two-year-old and an infant. I think now that I was suffering from baby blues or postpartum depression. I was angry at my husband, who had moved us to a tiny mountain town and then abandoned us. I found myself with no friends or family or anyone I trusted to talk to, learn from, be comforted by. My life held no joy or purpose, just struggle from day to day to make it, and to put a good 'face' on it.

"I needed help—not just for my children, but for myself. I, too, was a child in need. *I* needed a 'village.' I had always been an overachiever, resilient, and a survivor, so I set about to put together what I needed. First, I put my babies in a stroller and pushed them down the hill three blocks to the public library. I made friends with the librarians. I talked with them and perhaps overstayed my welcome some days. I did this day after day—I dreaded the three-block push back up and up and up the very steep hill, with two children and several books in a stroller.

"Behind the library was a Methodist church. I joined. I'd never been a Methodist before, but it was close and it offered Mother's Day Out. I made friends with the director of Christian education, an older woman who had reared twins and a third child. Her stroller had been heavier than mine, and she was a very happy lady who had friends and activities to share.

"Before moving away from the city where I had taught at a university, I consulted a wise colleague about how to survive the move. 'You won't be happy until you take your life into your own hands and take care of yourself,' he said. 'You love teaching; go and find a job teaching there.'

"Empowered by this advice, I found the community college near the little town and introduced myself. I met an influential teacher who would become my mentor, advisor, oracle. She was a deal-maker and a truth-teller. Through her I was able to get a job as an instructor. In that setting, I found a place and a group of individuals—characters, fellow pilgrims, soul mates, companions. School, church, and the library became the familiar streets of my 'village.' I relied on support from these strong institutions, with their familiar patterns and rituals, to give balance and stability to my life, while I tried to make a home for my family in a big, empty house. As time went by, I added to the mix a series of projects, civic and professional.

"After years of building a life—often like a bird adding twig upon twig to make a nest for her babies—I found the strength through the support of new friends to master fear which at times had been paralyzing; to step out into the unknown and take creative risks; and to help prepare my children for life."

Clara's story is important. The parent who can do what she did models mastery over adversity and coping skills for her child. The benefits pass down to the next generation.

There is one other important aspect of having our children know they are part of a caring community: it integrates them into a diverse group of people beyond the family and lets them see that *what they do matters*. Being part of a community helps children fulfill their needs for belonging and develop empathy, a sense of gratitude, and the concept of self-sacrifice. This is an extremely valuable lesson. We do not always have to focus on trying to make it easy for our children as a protection against rough times; again, preparation is the watchword, and allowing our children awareness of the pain and suffering that exists in the world, and offering them opportunities to help, strengthens them.

As parents, we need to take the long view: seeing parenting through the lens of a telescope, not a microscope. We need to understand our whole life; where our parenting comes from; what kind of parents our parents were and what they taught us while we were their disciples. And who taught them? We need the whole picture. Stated another way, handling a specific question from a child or an important event in the child's life is great, but it is not looking at parenting through the widest lens possible.

This means that some of our cherished beliefs and concepts may have to go. Sometimes we have to eradicate old misunderstandings about what it means to parent wisely, handed down by well-intentioned but misguided ancestors. Often we have dragged outmoded emotional baggage around for years without opening it up to see if there might be newer and better information available.

Noted clinical psychologist Dr. Leonard Holmes has suggested that "life metaphors" can shape how we live. He points out that as children, we need to understand and organize our world, and we begin to develop metaphors. Think of the brain as a filing cabinet, and of childhood as the time when we open the files and put labels on them, based on our environment at that time. Holmes points out that we often spend the rest of our lives putting new material in these files, and, I would add, as parents we must remove some old, outdated files—empty our emotional filing cabinet of material that causes us pain or holds us back. And, we have to add some new files.

The risk for parents who do not take time for reflection upon their own history, feelings, and motives is that they may become crippled, fearful, and vulnerable to manipulation and abuse by their children. The promise of "good-enough parenting" is that you get your life back, along with a sense of freedom, peace, strength, and courage. Is there a risk in working towards understanding how we got to be the way we are? What's the cost? What do we have to lose?

We lose our feelings of being in control and of exaggerated importance. If we don't grow along with our children and learn from them, we can maintain the illusion of central position and can hold on to our familiar role of authority and of being right because we are the parents who already know everything.

One of the struggles we have as parents is finding the balance between self-nurturing and selfishness; between self-care and self-centeredness. One way of looking at these concepts is to see them not as either/or. Life is not a matter of being here or there, but rather the freedom of living in a both/and universe.

It is well and good to be able to answer questions such as "Where do babies come from?" or "Why do people have to die?" But being a good parent—a master teacher with something invaluable to teach our young apprentices and disciples—is much more than being right or wrong in a given situation. It is much more than whether one is strict or permissive around curfews, believes in giving children allowances, or is for or against belly-button piercing. The *whole being* of the parent is what the child picks up on. One of the best gifts we can bestow on our children is to keep trying our best and knowing that our best will be good enough.

When a child is born, two people are turned into role models instantly, whether they like it or not. "An inadvertent example" is how psychologist Lawrence Balter describes what a parent becomes without even trying, because a child is watching and learning. Anna Quindlen argues that parents ought to modify their behavior when elevated to the position of parent.

There is a thriving subculture of parents who act as if everything goes on as it did before they had children. Quindlen pronounces this attitude "ridiculous." Having children, she says, "changes everything. Or at least it ought to."

Years earlier, Linda Weltner, writing in the *Boston Globe*, said, "Parents, like everyone else, find their inner strength faltering under pressure, their optimism flickering at crucial moments. We talk so much about what goes wrong, so little about what goes right. Yet, the testimony from children speaking with gratitude about the kind of parenting they received slowly mounts. And the parents who emerge, it is comforting to know, often had grievous faults, or endured great personal misfortune, yet their children came away from childhood affirming life."

The good-enough parent believes that what we dream for our children, we have hope of attaining for ourselves. This is the gift of parenthood—the gift our children bestow on us.

lesson eight

The Knack of Being Happy through Major Life Transitions

> Fear is the cheapest room in the house.
> I would like to see you living
> In better conditions . . .
>
> —HAFIZ

What are life transitions? They are part of a process we all go through. Separation anxiety, empty-nest syndrome, midlife crisis are names given to some major life transitions. They challenge our sense of invulnerability or immortality. To the universe, our big life transitions are less than a footnote. Knowing and accepting this gives us opportunities to reflect, to detach from the particular experience and to assess our situation. Transitions allow us to make mid-course corrections as needed and help keep us from being blindly driven. Transitions also provide opportunities for us to look at stages of individuality unfolding.

When we do not take the transitions of life so seriously, recognizing that everyone has them, it lightens our load. We realize that we are part of a process of development that comes and goes. We can decide to participate in the process with integrity, to live with passion, without going off the rails. The fun comes in knowing that we are not in control. Hafiz says that to make it through life's journey we must be light, happy, and free to go dancing. When we let go of negative attitudes and unnecessary attachments, we are free to "travel light, dwell deep," as my Celtic priest friend says.

It is important to remember that the forces of nature have made us. Knowing this, we need not despair over life's major transitions which move us along on our journey. Listen again to Hafiz: "I wish I could show you / When you are lonely or in darkness / The Astonishing Light / Of your own Being."

49

Teddy Bears

"I'M NEVER GOING TO GET RID OF THIS TEDDY BEAR," five-year-old Caleb said with absolute certainty. He was busy at the time preparing for a major venture into foreign territory: he was beginning kindergarten.

"I know," his mother said, nodding. "Teddy is special to you."

Caleb stood resolute in the center of the room, holding the scuffed, worn, one-eyed, wobbly-legged bear. "Even when I'm grown up and married I'm still going to keep this teddy."

"Of course," his mother said. "Teddy has been a very special friend and we don't just throw away special friends."

"I don't want him on the bed anymore, but I'll put him on this shelf by my bookcase," the boy said.

One of the major tasks of a young child is the management of separation anxiety. It is not something that we can cure. But once we face our anxiety, understand it, and deal with it, we feel a sense of mastery. Mastery is subjective and internal. Major life decisions which create opportunities for growth often require separation from former support systems. At each stage of development in our lives, mastery becomes important.

Caleb's mother remembered his first week at nursery school. When she had come to pick him up, his teacher mentioned that several children, including her little one, had had "accidents."

Wet pants had been exchanged for dry ones and no one had made a fuss. On the way home, Caleb had asked his mother if she would sing "I Like You How You Are" to him. She sang the words from one of Mr. Rogers' songs which obviously had special meaning for him on this occasion: "I like you as you are / I wouldn't want to change things / Or even rearrange things / Not by far. . . ."

The developmental steps we take often require that we risk what was most precious to us at the previous phase. One of the constant challenges in this process is the management of separation anxiety, which begins early in life. A child's "leaving home" is a developmental phase for the parent as well as for the child—no matter at what age the leaving occurs.

There had been other clues that beginning kindergarten created some special anxieties, and not only about Teddy. Caleb was insistent that he be taught how to tie his shoelaces and zip his jacket the weekend before the first kindergarten day. He was less than reassured by his mother's comments that many children do not know how to tie their shoelaces when they begin kindergarten.

"And I think I like Daddy better than I like you," he stated matter-of-factly as he worked on his shoelaces.

"That's all right," his mother said, trying to hide the sharp twinge his words brought. "Lots of times boys your age begin to feel that way."

He looked at her and said, "I know it sounds like I don't like you at all, but I really do, but only a little bit right now."

"Why must mothers always be seen as the villains?" she wondered as she gave Caleb a hug. "Please don't worry about it," she said. "However much you love me now is enough."

"Could I have a piece of your jewelry to keep?" he asked her the night before school began. Together they selected an inexpensive brooch that had been a favorite gift since her college days.

"I'll keep it in my room forever," he said as he placed the piece of jewelry in a small wooden box on his bookshelf reserved for precious, secret things.

The first few days of school passed quickly. Caleb was feeling good about himself. As his mother tucked him in bed, he whispered in her ear, "I think I like you and Daddy equally both the same."

Caleb, like most children, managed the anxiety associated with separation with a minimum of difficulty. He mastered a fear and learned something important about coping. For some children, however, the threat of the loss of their mother is extremely frightening and stressful. Often for mothers, it is a painful and baffling experience. As the young child grows and matures, he will be asked to risk separation again and again for new horizons yet to be defined. And so will his parents.

The years passed quickly and the once-vivid memories began to blur for Caleb's mom, only to return in clear focus at special times of remembering. Like watching him begin his first year of middle school—a new school district, new classmates, travel by bus.

"I'm not hungry this morning," the usually ravenous twelve-year-old said. "I'm really nervous about the new school."

"Most people are nervous when they're starting something new," his mother reassured him. "Are you nervous in general, or is there something in particular that's bothering you?"

"Just two things," he said. "I don't know if the kids are taking their notebooks the first day, and I wonder if I'll see any kids I know. It would be easier going in with some kids I know."

His mother was relieved that his concerns were so specific, so easily addressed.

"Suppose I give you a lift today?" she offered. "We can wait in the car until you see some people you know; if they don't have notebooks, you can leave yours in the car if you'd like."

"Thanks, Mom," he said. "And could you hurry up the scrambled eggs and two pieces of toast? We're going to be late."

The automobile had barely come to a stop when the car door opened. "I thought you wanted to wait for some kids you know," she said.

"I already see three," he said as he slammed the door. "And they don't have notebooks."

Later that week his mother helped him pick up his room a bit. Opening the closet door, she noticed the tiny box "for special, precious things" almost hidden behind a football and several electronic games. She hadn't thought about the brooch or about the stuffed bear in years. She couldn't resist a peek.

The tarnished brooch lay amid coins, shells, and other small unidentified pieces of a child's treasure. And on the highest shelf of the closet, perched in a safe out-of-the-way place, sat Teddy, looking down, with his one eye, on his kingdom.

Worn and torn, with stuffing peeking out, black nose loose, and shortened red tongue, once snipped with scissors by an active three-year-old, Teddy was an eloquent reminder that when stressful times in our lives occur, all of us get by, each in his or her own way, with a little help from our friends.

50

Normal Adolescence: Go Away Closer

"Go away closer" is one of my favorite concepts for understanding the push-pull on teenagers dealing with issues of dependency and autonomy. Adolescence is a period of major transition. This period in our children's lives is confusing and scary for parents who wonder if there is such a thing as *normal* adolescence. For me, the answer is a resounding "yes."

"What does normal adolescence look like?" Frankie's mother asked me. I told her that normal adolescence is like a house that is being remodeled. The walls are out; there's plaster dust and rubble all about, but construction is going on. Something is going to emerge with a keen resemblance to the past structure but hopefully bigger, better, and more functional.

There can be great discomfort in having to live with the house while the remodeling is taking place. Adolescence is not a neat, tidy period, but it is not the mess of remodeling that makes for *abnormality*. The danger is if the construction stops, if some sense of progress is not visible in the midst of the dust and rubble, or if there is so much tearing down that the house caves in.

The task for the wise parent is to understand that the adolescent is involved in a major remodeling process and to support efforts to build on the past—to help the floundering child keep the foundation without destroying it totally.

"How do I protect this kid from himself?" Frankie's mother wondered. "I have a child who won't even bother to tie his shoelaces and still sucks his thumb asking me why I'm so eager to keep him dependent on me! One day he can't figure out how to wash his socks and the next day he's ready to move out!"

Go away closer.

The adolescent remodeling process has to do with identity consolidation. What is my house going to look like? How will I and others view it when it's completed? Sometimes it feels as though what is going to emerge is not going to turn out; it's going to be wrong; it won't be worth all the effort. Some adolescents give up working on the remodeling, feel defeated, feel that the price is too high, become embittered and alienated—any of which can lead to depression.

It's easier to live with the old building, even though it has been outgrown. But the normal adolescent does not give in to the temptation to quit. Instead, she or he rises to the task with varying needs for support and consultation. Normal adolescents do the remodeling. They do it with some sense of loss, for in the process the familiar, comfortable old house gives way to new surroundings.

Frankie did not succumb. He struggled with his parents' unwillingness to grant him total independence at age fifteen, while accepting their support for pursuing his impressive academic and intellectual goals. It seemed to his parents that each week brought a new challenge.

"Frankie is no more," his mother told me with her most solemn expression. "Our son now responds to us only if we call him Frank. Any slip on our part is proof to him that we absolutely do not want him to grow up."

As a friend of his family, I followed Frankie's adolescent journey. I watched his parents struggle with the dependence-independence tightrope they walked with their gifted child. I watched the mediating effects of humor as they supported this transition.

His mom admitted she felt embarrassed that her son had been the only child in his elementary school class who would not tie his shoelaces. "The best thing about middle school for me," she said with a grin, "is that *nobody* ties their sneakers!"

Some adolescents prefer the status quo they have established to the possibilities a new house can offer. Some are too vulnerable to the expectations and comments of others who view the progress and pass judgment on the quality of the work. Sometimes the adolescent builder has trouble asking for help on his or her project, fearing that control of the project will be lost. Sometimes there is a tug-of-war with the former landlords over ownership, which can threaten the adolescent's efforts towards independent, autonomous living.

Staying with the house-building metaphor, how does the growing adolescent hold on to what is good and needed from the past while building for the future? How does he love his parents while preserving a sense of autonomy and not feeling too dependent?

"You won't believe Frank's latest proposal," his mother said. "He has talked to his high school counselor and researched a program for early admission to Harvard. He wants to skip his senior year in high school." His parents became willing to support Frank's decision. "His father did tell him that he'd have to stop sucking his thumb before the interview with the college admissions board. For me, I'm rejoicing that Frank has discovered loafers."

What does the adolescent need in order to complete the renovation process with a minimum of distress? He or she needs support for separation and individuation issues, the resolution of which is part of the remodeling of the old structure. The adolescent needs guidance so that the project is not viewed as too mammoth, does not become unrealistic, too overwhelming, or too expensive. Adolescents need access to good adult builders and remodelers who can help them to become master architects of their own lives. They need adults who can respect the enormous effort involved, admire the restructuring, and anticipate with pleasure the finished product.

This means that we parents must hold out a sense of purpose and meaning to adolescents, affirming the importance of their remodeling task, the difficulty of the work required, approaching the adolescent builder with utmost care and respect.

Frank was accepted to Harvard at the end of his junior year in high school and graduated with honors. His parents had made their own transitions as they supported Frank's journey. Frank had been right when at age fourteen he outlined his abilities to function "perfectly well" on his own, but acknowledged his need for continued support from his parents.

Go away closer is an important concept for teenagers and parents. It's difficult for parents to achieve, but it is possible. Doing it can make all the difference. When you are tempted to go ballistic over your adolescent's efforts, try to remember: it isn't easy being an adolescent remodeler. So, if you know one, be kind to him or her, support the renovation effort, and, when the opportunity presents itself, step up and lend a hand.

51

Rites of Passage: How Do You Get There from Here?

"Where did I go wrong?" a client asked when her daughter came home from her first semester in college with her tongue and belly button pierced and a large tattoo on her ankle. I thought about how easily parents blame themselves. "Chances are this isn't about anything you did wrong," I answered. But the question she posed set me thinking about how, in the absence of communities where the elders create rites of passage, kids create their own.

We all long for an outward and visible sign of our inner state or experience. Perhaps my client's daughter was announcing that she now belonged to a larger group of peers outside her family. Tongue-piercing says, "I'm initiated, free from the past, and ready to go!" But where? It's a question Alice in Wonderland asked the Cheshire Cat. "Could you tell me which path I should take?"

"That depends a good deal on where you want to go," said the cat.

"I don't really know," said Alice.

"Then clearly, any path will do!"

When people are adrift, like Alice, they often discover that what looked like Wonderland isn't so wonderful. So long as they get *somewhere,* any way will do. A tattoo or body piercing for its own sake has no real or lasting value. In some cultures it has deep collective significance. It connects the individual to an ancient heritage. For a college freshman away from home for the first time, it expresses individuality and alienation.

I think of rites of passage as milestones to keep us from getting lost. Ancient Roman road builders provided signposts for soldiers going out. They knew that without these large stone markers, their mighty legions could get lost. Similarly, we need society's help in providing the milestones that guide and direct those who come behind us, to show them the sure and safe way to go. Biology and society provide some—like menses, driver's license, dating age—but these are not uniform. When we do not provide designated rites of passage, our kids make up their own.

Bidden or unbidden, understood or not, we *will* experience rites of passage. The question is how much attention we will pay, how conscious we will be of their true meaning—which has to do with connections and belonging. Is the benefit worth the cost?

In American culture we tend to downplay the importance of the rites and rituals that mark the transition from one life stage to another. Often, we relegate them to churches, to initiation into sororities and fraternities, and to social events, especially parties. While there is nothing wrong with parties as part of celebrating, they are only one part of a larger whole. Something more lasting, more deeply resonant, is required to connect us to the greater flow of the generations.

It is human nature to yearn to be initiated into a group, to be recognized and accepted. Body piercing, tattoos, school cliques, street gangs, or cults are attempts at meeting this deep need. In the absence of positive communal ceremonies and recognition, however, they have the opposite effect. They result in the confusion and meaninglessness that the Cheshire Cat described when he explained to Alice that if she didn't much care where she got to, it didn't matter which way she went. If "the way" doesn't matter, what we do, how we behave, doesn't matter.

The way didn't seem to matter to the seventeen-year-old high school senior who sat beside me on a plane to Cancun. Looking bored and tired as she fastened her seat belt, she said to her teenage friend on the other side of her, "I need a drink. I don't mean water, either. I need a strong alcoholic beverage right now!" I looked at my watch. It was 9:20 a.m. As I talked with her I learned that she was making her first trip to Mexico—without her family—to celebrate her upcoming eighteenth birthday and to be a part of the "Girls Gone Wild" scene. This milestone seemed to be missing any sense of heritage, of enlightenment, of mystery, of wonder. What could her parents be thinking? Without guidance from a strong family-community connection, she is at risk to fall down the rabbit hole.

Who can help our children meet their belonging needs when parents' needs aren't met either? If we have not done our own psychological work, we cannot expect our children to excel in this task. Our young people need help when the balance of power shifts between them and their parents. Where can young adults go for support and recognition when they become decision-makers and begin to take responsibility for their own lives? While some societies mentor their young through their teen years, we often treat this important life passage as though it is an extended illness to be endured until it passes.

Helping the young person assume the role of adult is critical. When this task is accomplished in a healthy way, the mature adult does not want to go back to childhood. Rites, rituals, and public markers contribute to a healthy, happy, meaningful life.

There are rites of passage moments for all of us, no matter our age: baby blessings and naming; coming-of-age initiations; marriage and joining; divorce and parting; midlife; old age; death. How can we honor such moments?

When I was sixty-nine I began talking about retirement from my career. I had knowledge about the event and had helped others through it. Now it was my turn. My transition was speeded up unexpectedly when I fell off a curb and broke my ankle.

My closest friends decided to "help" me in this transition by hosting a retirement party. "You can't back out after we go public," they teased.

Retirement was a rite of passage that needed to be acknowledged, honored, and celebrated by friends who supported and cared for me. It was a public acknowledgment of a long and complex process.

A rite of passage involves letting go of the past and acknowledging publicly that we are moving in a new direction. No matter what our age, rites of passage can keep us on course during critical times of change. They help us know who we are and to anticipate who we will become.

52

So You Want to Be a Grown-up?

THE STORY GOES THAT A YOUNG COLLEGE GRADUATE knocked on the door of the world and said, "Hello, world, I'm Jane Doe, A.B." The world replied, "Come in, Jane, and I'll teach you the other twenty-four letters of the alphabet."

In moving from adolescence into young adulthood, there is much to learn, including the achievement of a male or female social role, getting started in an occupation, taking on civic responsibility, and learning to live in significant relationships. For many it involves marriage and child rearing.

The primary task of the young adult is the separation of authentic self from family expectations—real and imagined. Young adulthood (usually seen as ages twenty-two to thirty-four) is a time of preparing for taking one's place in the world. Young adults leave home and find that the world is difficult. Life never again will be like it was. Their task is to go and create a new life—*their* life. This process requires testing their moral compass to find out what they truly value. For some, this time of testing leads to excess, with painful consequences. The healthy young adult gradually learns to set limits and comes to self-awareness without doing irreparable damage.

Young adults face the uneasy task of exploring, of breaking the rules, or testing the waters, without running amok. They learn, for example, they can take an individual stance against family without destroying either themselves or their family relationships. As a college graduate in the late 1950s trying to find my own moral compass, I worked for the Southern Regional Council on Human Relations in Atlanta, a clearinghouse for efforts towards racial integration of the South. My parents were segregationists of the old school—that's just the way it is and is supposed to be, end of discussion.

I told my parents that I worked at the Southern Regional Council and they did not question what I did, because once they found the offices were located in a Methodist church, they made the assumption that the organization was church-related and that made it okay. This was my first major break from the family rules, and being set apart was painful. I wanted to set my own standards, establish my own sense of right and wrong, but I did not want to lose the relationship I had with my parents. I knew that risk was involved and that I had to be prepared to take responsibility for the path I had chosen, a path that, at the time, set me apart from every member of my family. My decision was not fueled by anger or rebellion, but by an awareness that this break was necessary if I was to be true to myself.

Young people have to make hard choices. It takes courage to take responsibility for one's life and to speak out. There is often a price to be paid, but for me the best prices I've paid have been ones that flowed from conscious choices I've made, acknowledging the risk involved.

Young adults must address issues of sexual morality and sexual orientation and come to some kind of resolve about how to make a living, how to function in the world and to understand and cope with the secret, intimate areas of their lives. This is a time when they need a community, a sense of safety and belonging and self-worth within the parameters of this stage. If there is no mastery of this phase, then the uncertainty will add to the emotional baggage dragged to the next phase. What is needed is a new kind of interdependence, a new sense of belonging, a new sense of what it means to be fully human.

Parents have little or no control of the young adult, but if the seeds have been planted along the way, if parents have given helpful advice and education in small doses, the young adult will have already developed some inner resources. And the parent can still be an advisor and role model. Nonetheless, parental support has to be solicited by the young adult. A parent who imposes his or her will, who overreacts, is judgmental, or who panics easily, will not be effective. Sometimes the solution for parents of young adults is to reclaim more of their own individuality—to enjoy life too much to spend useless time worrying about what the young adult is doing.

I agree with Freud's proposition that good mental health is determined by the ability to love and to work. Love has to include love of oneself and of humanity. Work is most satisfying and fulfilling when it is seen as an extension of oneself and is imbued with meaning and purpose. It is important for emerging adults to seek this balance.

Psychoanalyst Erik Erikson saw the young adult conflict as "intimacy versus isolation." Many young adults marry in hope of finding in the other a sense of completeness that they have not been able to integrate. But the young adult's effort to find himself or herself in someone else is doomed to failure. According to Erikson, one cannot establish a true sense of intimacy until he or she has established a sense of identity. The major task of young adulthood—that of building a secure internal identity—is a process that takes patience, dedication, trust and courage. It is a building block for the next stage of life.

Midlife Crisis

"I've never paid much attention to age before," my niece said after her forty-fifth birthday. "But being on the downside of forty does give me pause."

Middle age—or midlife—is loosely defined as the period between young adulthood and old age, roughly the period between forty and sixty. What constitutes midlife is different for different people. We know midlife has hit when we wake up one morning and think, "I'm going to be such and such an age in a few days and I just can't be, won't be, *that* old." When this happens, we are experiencing our own version of midlife crisis.

We stereotypically define midlife crisis as the male approaching fifty who dumps his mate, buys a flashy convertible, and runs off with a younger woman. Or we think of parents whose grown or nearly grown children move out, leaving them with an "empty nest." This midlife crisis, especially critical for mothers, is one of the major transitions in the individuation process. For some, their particular crisis may be more subtle. But midlife crises are inevitable—they come to us all, so we would do well to get ourselves ready.

What creates midlife crises for many of us is that we stop seeing the future in terms of our potential and begin to see it in terms of our limitations. "I can't start a new career at this age." "I won't have the energy to pursue this dream." For women, the midlife crisis frequently is tied to reproductive decisions: "The biological clock has run out and I can't have children." For men, midlife issues often focus on physical changes and concerns about sexual performance, generating fear and anxiety and a lot of lamentable behavior.

The issue in dealing with the midlife crisis is whether our decisions and behaviors come from conscious awareness, or whether we act out without considering the consequences. There is a price to pay. Knowing that and being willing to pay the price—to accept the consequences—enables us to make life changes without regret. Before we take action we can ask ourselves "Why am I making this career change?" "Why am I seeking a divorce?" "What do I want?" "Who will be hurt?" "Is there another way to get what I need?"

One of the issues involved in midlife struggles is the fear of death—and the fear of never having lived. We all know people who kick over the traces—have an affair, spend recklessly, run away—and then regret it. At every crisis point in our lives, there is the temptation to engage in risky behaviors in an attempt to solve the problems inherent in this particular life passage. At midlife, the need to feel vital and alive leads many people to act out sexually, drink excessively, or spend beyond their means.

A midlife crisis presents us with a dangerous opportunity. It provides us the chance for change and growth as well as the risk of regression or stagnation. The danger of midlife is real. Successful transition to the next life stage is not guaranteed.

In midlife, our agenda changes, moving from differentiation to integration. My own midlife crisis came at age fifty, when I made the agonizing decision to end a twenty-year marriage. This move, painful at the time, gave me the opportunity to become more creative and more alive. It was a leap of faith at the time, but I look back on the decision as a necessary move toward authenticity.

To dye one's hair red in midlife as a statement about not becoming stagnant is a choice without serious consequences. To choose a divorce requires factoring in pain not only for oneself but for others, including children. My decision to rear a child as a single parent was difficult. Having done the conscious work necessary did not mean I avoided the pain and hurt. But understanding what the price would be and being ready to pay it did make it possible not to be saddled with regret and bitterness.

Many of my clients tell me that at midlife, it dawns on them that all the activity, all the piling up of money, all the fancy homes and cars have done nothing to prevent the arrival of the grim reaper. At that point, they have to sort through what they are doing that works and what does not. They have to come to grips with what *truly* matters to them. For some of us, the truth hits us in the face like a bucket of cold water.

Turning fifty was very difficult for a client who, years earlier, had married someone much younger. "I was scared that at age fifty I'd wake up and look like Grandma Moses and he wouldn't love me anymore. I saw myself as a vulnerable tiny flower with a huge slug eating away at me. Now at age sixty I see myself as a beautiful lotus flower, with just a tiny aphid."

It is during midlife that we can look at our fears and worries as bricks we have been dragging. Maybe it's anger and bitterness over broken relationships, a career path not chosen, health issues. If we try, we can recognize symptoms of a heavy heart and identify the prison holding us in. There is a proverb that says midlife is the old age of youth and the youth of old age. If this is true, then at this point in our lives we all get to stand on the threshold of a new youth, what Gail Sheehy, author of the book *Passages*, calls the "second adulthood."

Erikson defines the developmental task of middle age as generativity versus stagnation. Healthy middle-aged adults are producing, performing meaningful work, engaging in healthy relationships, redefining their lives, and addressing what works for them. Others become stagnant and inactive, negative and fearful. In a word, they become *stuck*. Getting unstuck involves seeing this crisis as normal, seeking insight and awareness, and confronting the pain of letting go of what might have been in order to change and grow. Living into the exciting generative potential of this developmental phase allows us to rid ourselves of some of the bricks we've been dragging and gets us ready for the next transition—to old age.

54

The Promise of Old Age

WHEN HER UNCLE DIED, one thirteen-year-old came face to face with her own mortality for the first time. "How can people live knowing they're just going to die?" she asked her mother.

"The trick is to live your life every day, making the best of it. Then, when the time comes, you'll be ready," her mother assured her. "You can believe me when I tell you that your inner strength will grow and grow." The child believed her and was comforted.

Those of us who have made the transitions from childhood through adulthood and middle age now find ourselves in the "old age" category, delicately referred to as "Seniors." This last stage of life begins somewhere between the 50-plus eligibility for AARP and the 65-plus discount tickets at the cinema. For most people, it lasts a long time. For many, including myself, it is the best time of all. "Leen, do you feel old?" my godson asked me on my sixty-fifth birthday.

"No, I don't," I replied honestly. "Why do you ask?"

"Well, you don't look old and you don't act old, so I just wondered if you felt old." I found the question intriguing. I had never paid much attention to age, but I was keenly aware that Medicare had now claimed me as one of its own.

As old people, we have a choice to make: we can live in fear or we can accept and embrace. Every day we have the opportunity to make the best of what we do have. But we cannot do this if we haven't lived the life within us, if we're all clogged up. We can take medication for blocked arteries, but how do we unclog our spirit? A lot of smart people have tried to convey the secrets of a joyful, meaningful old age. Carl Jung tells us that your vision will become clear "only when you can look into your own heart." An old Hasidic saying reassures us that "If you carry your own lantern, you need not fear darkness."

In psychologist Erik Erikson's theory, reaching this stage is a good thing, but not accepting it suggests that earlier problems retarded our development. The task of old age is to develop ego integrity, with a minimal amount of despair. Ego integrity means coming to terms with your life. It means facing rather than denying the difficulties of old age. It means looking back and accepting the course of events, the choices made, your life as you've lived it. It means acknowledging and grieving that your body is failing, as is your memory.

One who approaches death without fear has wisdom. This kind of wisdom does not mean that one is necessarily intellectually gifted. People in their declining years have taught me a great deal by their simple and gentle approach to life and death and by their generosity of spirit.

Pop Barefoot was such a model. Facing death from cancer and paralyzing strokes, he allowed friends and neighbors who wanted to visit him to come and sit at his feet while he reclined in his living room. He often cracked jokes, and guests would leave laughing while he wasted away. He took comfort in the belief that he was helping people by allowing them to face their secret fears about life and death. He was a role model, not just of how to die, but how to live. He saw life as both funny and sacred, and years after his death, his humorous take on life, as well as his reverence for it, is still remembered.

For many, old age begins when they realize that they are now the oldest member of the family, the oldest at the table, the one continuing to survive. Their focus changes. Retirement is usually a major part of it. Retirement is a time of having more choices. My favorite view of retirement is an inward retiring from competitiveness, having less need to say what I know, and a desire for more options, more opportunities to pursue what I feel passionate about. This final stage of life can be full of depth and breadth, if we have done our work and successfully transitioned through the earlier stages. My elderly friend wrote in her Christmas card, "I continue to love books but try not to buy many. I am at the stage where I would rather give away than to add to my collections. That is a good place in life to be. Every age has its rewards, doesn't it?"

Self-knowledge and awareness take work. The difficulties of old age are not to be dismissed or sugar-coated. They are *very* real for the older adult and for caregivers. But the promise of old age is that as the body gives way, the spirit grows. Loss and discovery go hand in hand. We can set the example, be a model for those coming behind us. We *will* be models, whether we want to or not. We can be models for discontent, bitterness, and remorse, or for acceptance, dignity, joy, and serenity. It matters profoundly what we choose. If you are not old yet, look around and find people who have made it and learn from them. Learn what they know, and when you get to that place you will find that physical loss, including memory, is a price worth paying for the incredible clarity you receive about what is truly important in life.

lesson nine

The Knack of Being Happy in the Face of Death

One regret, dear world,
That I am determined not to have
When I am lying on my deathbed
Is that
I did not kiss you enough.

—HAFIZ

Life and death together weave the tapestry of life—they are threads in the same fabric, from the beginningless beginning to the endless end. Before I was a zygote, I was a sperm and an egg—both living somewhere. My friend's grandmother, facing her own death, said to her granddaughter, "I'm not afraid to die because I've figured something out. I probably was very happy somewhere before I was born, and wherever it was, I bet I didn't want to leave. But life has turned out to be okay, so I know that even though I don't much want to leave, where I'm going will be okay, too."

I have worked professionally with hundreds of people facing their own death or the death of a loved one. I have been there to support them on this journey and I have been privileged to witness incredible strength, courage, dignity, and grace in the face of death. I can promise the reader that it is possible to survive and derive great wisdom—and yes, even joy—from such experiences. It is not easy to come to this place, and we do not do it on our own. We come to it little by little. We learn from loved ones who go before us.

Children and adults alike can benefit when we see death as a seamless part of life that knits us together and gives our lives meaning and purpose. Our children will be just as afraid and horrified by death as we are. But talking comfortably about death, answering questions honestly and modeling acceptance of death as a natural process, is a blessing we give our children. Best of all, we provide the example of one who is aware that life is all the more precious because it is going to end.

55

The Job of a Lifetime

IN THE LATE 1930S, IN A TINY HOSPITAL ROOM—which had only a bed, a small white metal table, and a chair—my family stood crying around the bed in which I lay. I was six years old and was not expected to survive diphtheria. Often semiconscious, I could hear their voices but I could not make out what they were saying. I remember their tears. And my mother's hands on my feet, as she stood at the foot of my bed. Later, when I was more lucid, I remember my five-year-old sister, Gloria, standing by my bed holding the coleus I had rooted and planted in a coffee can. She had whacked the plant off and stood holding it over my face. "Here," she said, "I brought you a flower."

Recovery was a long, slow, tedious process, complicated by bouts of jaundice, whooping cough, measles, and chicken pox. This very early near-death experience was the signature event of my life. It marked me, changed me, made me see the world from a perspective my family and friends did not, *could not*, understand. I did not see angels or light at the end of a tunnel or hear heavenly music, as many others report. But I was consciously *aware* that it is good to be alive; that life is worth living; that it is full of miraculous surprises; that I am fortunate, blessed, cared for. That experience has never left me. It has seen me through poverty, struggles, divorce, and tragedy. I just know that life is as it should be, even if I die. And I'm happy to be here!

I also learned very early in life that when death comes to call, it is no respecter of age. I was twelve, and my sister Ruth only twenty-nine, when she died of cancer. I was alone with her in the dimly lit hospital room as she took her last breath. Many years later, a friend listened to this story I shared. "How could your parents have left you alone through that? You were just a child."

Another friend said with great tenderness, "I invite you to consider that this was a traumatic experience for you." I understood their concern, and yes, the experience *was* very traumatic for me. But it remains a profound one that I would never want to change.

We cannot talk about death without talking about suffering. *The Interrupted Life* recounts the story of Etty Hillesum, who was in a Nazi concentration camp by conscious choice. She preferred to work and help people in the camp rather than accept the privilege of being a translator for the Nazis. Having a spiritual awakening herself, she set about bringing an enlightened attitude, courage, and a sense of meaning and purpose to life for those on their way to the gas chambers, including herself. She perished there. Her memoir survived and should be required reading, along with *The Diary of Anne Frank*. We learn from the examples of history.

In my years of work with adults dealing with unresolved grief, I have seen firsthand the terrible effects of secrecy about death. Clients have suffered years of pain and sadness over some significant loss they were not allowed to grieve. One twenty-seven-year-old client had always felt that she was incomplete, that some part of her was missing. She couldn't understand the feeling, and she couldn't make it go away. It was only when her parents finally told her that she had had an identical twin sister who died shortly after birth that this made sense. Having this information, she was able to locate her sister's grave, visit it, grieve, and move on. Her parents had sought to protect her by withholding this painful information. We learn from truth.

Claudia was a successful businesswoman who knew only that her mother had passed away when she was nine. Her family wanted to shield her from the ugly details. She came home from school and was simply told that her mother had died, and was at the funeral home. She was not allowed to see the body or attend the funeral. For years afterward Claudia carried a huge weight of sadness, confusion, and guilt. Perhaps she had done something bad that had led to her mother's death and her family was shielding her, she said to me, tears streaming down her face. Through our work together, Claudia was able to confront her father and insist on knowing how her mother died and why she was not allowed to speak of her.

Finally, she learned that her mother had committed suicide and the family had kept this secret. In the light of truth, Claudia could begin to cope with her own life. One of the most moving experiences I have had in such situations occurred when Claudia wrote a letter to her long-departed mother, forgiving her and telling her how much she loved her. We both cried as Claudia read this letter aloud at her last session with me.

We are as sick as the secrets we keep. We do a disservice to children when we overprotect, when we separate death from life. If we lock death away like a deep, dark secret, it can make us—and our children—sick. Children need to witness the emotional bonding, the sadness over loss, the celebration of a life lived. If we shelter children from these experiences, we rob them of natural opportunities to experience deep feelings and intense bonding. Robbed of such opportunities, many youngsters find cheap substitutes that are detrimental to their emotional growth—and ours.

56

When Children Face Grief

IN MY CLINICAL PRACTICE, I HAVE SPENT literally thousands of hours dealing with unresolved pain, anger, and guilt that did not find expression as grief at the time of a loss. I have counseled clients, taught courses, given workshops, and published on issues of loss and grief. After I lost my sister to cancer, as an adult I grieved the loss of a brother to colon cancer and the loss of another brother and both parents to heart disease. But one is never fully prepared for death. Despite all my training and life experiences, I was knocked sideways by the untimely death of a beloved friend, the mother of my twin godchildren.

Janie and Nathan lost their mother suddenly when they were fourteen. As a clinician, teacher, mother, friend, and godmother I share our story, with their permission. We hope it will help others. My godchildren were nine when their parents decided to move from Boston to North Carolina. Their mother, Laura, urged me to sell my home and come with them. I had been divorced for several years and my son was in college in Georgia, where I grew up.

"Live with us in an in-law apartment and we'll take care of you in your old age," she said. "Tim has three more years in the army, and you can help me with the kids when he's away. You will be in a university town, so you can teach and you know they'll need psychologists there. And anyway, Janie and Nathan won't leave if you don't come!"

We made the move together. Five years later, Laura was dead. Janie and Nathan were three weeks shy of their fifteenth birthday when they came home from school and found their thirty-eight-year-old mother in bed, having died in her sleep.

"Janie and Nathan were their mother's crowning achievement," the Episcopal priest said during the eulogy. She was right. The twins both faced indescribable pain, grief, and loss throughout the difficult, vulnerable season of adolescence. But in the end, they paid the price of suffering, and they triumphed.

The first stage in loss of a loved one is disbelief. Nathan was still grieving the death of his best friend, who had committed suicide four months earlier. "I don't believe this is happening to me; Mom wouldn't do this," Nathan sobbed in my arms. He had spent the night after his mother's death with a good friend next door. "When I woke up, I looked over and saw Joel in the same room we always sleep in and I thought 'Mom didn't die; it was just a bad dream.'"

It's not just children who feel that way. Their grandmother, when she learned by phone of her daughter's death, said later that she sat by the phone for a long time, waiting for a call back saying it was a mistake, that her daughter was alive. Disbelief may be nature's way of deadening the initial pain a little while we absorb the facts. It buys us a little time while we start to comprehend the truth. Short-term disbelief is often helpful. But prolonged disbelief can impede the grief process.

The priest came to our home the day before Laura's funeral to plan the service. Janie and Nathan, their father, and I made suggestions and requests regarding the service. It is important to give older children the opportunity to have some say in how things will go. This participation helps them begin to accept and believe. Janie and Nathan decided who they wanted to participate in the service and who they wanted to sit by, and their requests were honored.

"Leen, I don't want to do this," Janie whispered to me as we walked down the aisle of the church.

"Me, either," I said. "We'll get through this together." We sat on the front row and listened to their mother's close friend give a moving eulogy. Hundreds of people had filled the church, many of whom were Janie and Nathan's teachers. Nathan sat between me and his father, his hand in mine. As one of the readers moved to the lectern wearing heels, her ankle turned and she slipped momentarily. Nathan leaned over to me and whispered, "That's why I don't wear high heels." I squeezed his hand. "Your mom always loved your sense of humor," I whispered. Appropriate expressions of humor bode well at such times.

That night began a ritual that was to continue for several months. Nathan would arrive at my in-law apartment in their home with his sleeping bag and ask if he could sleep beside my bed. The answer was always yes. Soon, Janie would arrive, and they would talk until they could fall asleep. After several nights of this we shared a little laughter as I referred to the sleeping arrangements as a dorm, and suggested we have rules.

"What are the rules?" they asked.

"The only one I can think of right now is that your sleeping bags not block my path to the bathroom! If that happens, there will be severe consequences." They laughed at my mock seriousness.

"I feel like we've slept in your room before," Nathan said, "but I can't remember when."

"You did, when we lived in Boston. Remember when you were five and your house burned? You two and Mom and Papa lived with me for a while." They remembered then. "You two slept on either side of my bed in your sleeping bags."

We talked about that loss, about Janie's room being totally destroyed and the rest of the house being severely damaged by fire, smoke, and water. They recalled my taking them to Sears to buy pajamas and underwear, since their clothes were ruined. Most of all, they remembered the clothes and food that friends and church members delivered day after day. They remembered living in a condo for more than a year while the house was rebuilt. I reminded them of the lesson their mom had taught them about accepting help and support, and about not using personal tragedy as an excuse for poor attitude or behaviors. We talked about the gift their mother had given them in the way she supported them at that time when they were very afraid and anxious. Talking about that earlier loss and their mastery of that situation made it easier to get beyond the current pain.

Aiming for a light note on which to say good-night, I told them about my favorite memory from that earlier time when they slept in my room.

"The first night you were there," I told them, "Nathan woke up in the middle of the night, sat straight up, looked around the room and said, 'Leen, I really like this god-house!'"

"Well, you *were* my godmother, and that *was* your house!" We all laughed.

Nights were particularly tough times for the twins. Their father had to leave early in the morning for work, so he needed to say good-night before the twins' bedtime. Janie and Nathan stayed in their area of the house until their father retired and then they and their sleeping bags would arrive at my door. Often they curled up beside me in bed for a few minutes before the lights were turned out. Later, when I would hear one of them crying, I would get up and lie down beside them, stroking their back and temples until they fell asleep. It was during one of these times that Nathan voiced his wish to move away.

Running away is a common reaction. We desperately hope that some new face or some new person will take away the pain. If we give in to this urge for flight, the grief process does not run its course and we end up in big trouble.

Death and loss teach us that pain is a part of life and must be accepted if joy is also going to be a part of life. Parents and loved ones have a responsibility to help children see and understand that. They need to assure them that their feelings *will* change, that pain *will* diminish, and that healing *will* occur. We must let our children know that feeling deep sadness is a normal part of recovery. We must not encourage them to push away memories prematurely, just because they hurt so much.

There is no running away from death. It catches us all in the end. As adults, we must make time for our own grief. My own feelings of loss, betrayal, pain, anger, and sadness were as real as Janie's and Nathan's. When Laura died, my feelings found expression with the loving, understanding support of close friends and confidants, and in my writing. Several years later, my healing continues.

We must encourage children to voice *every* emotion, especially the negative ones.

"Do you think Mom can hear everything we're saying?" Janie asked me as she lay in my bed, her head on my shoulder. It was past midnight and she had been crying inconsolably for a long time.

"I think your mom would want you to say whatever you need to say that will make you feel better."

"You do? Are you sure?"

"Yes," I told her. "I'm very sure."

"Okay, then—I'm going to say that I am *really* mad at her for dying."

"I think your mom is very proud of you for letting her know how you're feeling. I think she's giving you a thumbs-up right now." We talked about our anger, sadness and loneliness. I held her close.

After a long while, Janie's tears stopped and she became very pensive. "Mom and I used to drive out to the beach and watch the dolphins. But I can't remember which bridge we stood on. Can you help me find it?"

We dressed quietly, slipped out of the house into the dark night, and took the fifteen-minute ride to the beach. We drove until she was sure she had located the bridge, and I pulled over for a few minutes as she told me of her visits there with her mother. I had not known about these.

"If you want me to bring you here again, I will, but if you want this to be a wonderful memory of something very special between you and your mom that you don't want to share, that's understandable." Janie thanked me, and we drove home. She never asked to return, but drove there alone when she was old enough.

Caring adults can help their children by answering all their questions, no matter how painful. "Leen, what do you think the autopsy will say?" Nathan asked me.

"I think that it will say that your Mom's death was caused by an accidental overdose of prescription drugs."

"I don't want it to say that," he said as we sat together on the stairs to my room.

I held him for a long time as we sat in silence. Nathan sat up, took my hand and, looking me in the eye, said, "Thanks. Now I want you to tell me straight up, do you think . . . ?" and the questions poured out, one after the other.

Sometimes children start to worry when memories begin to fade. It's scary when they can't remember specific things about their deceased parent. They need reassurance that this, too, is normal.

Several months after his mother's death, Nathan said to me, "I'm feeling really strange because I can't remember any more what Mom's voice sounded like."

"Your mom spoke with many voices," I said. "You may not remember how her voice *sounded*, but you can remember what her voice *taught* you and how it made you feel, especially when she said things that made you feel loved." Together we recalled such incidents; I would supply the words I remembered his mother saying, and Nathan would supply the feelings her words had created in him.

When a parent dies, young children often fear losing the parent who is still alive. Sometimes the remaining parent withdraws into his or her own pain and sorrow to the extent that—at least psychologically—the child has temporarily lost that parent, too. Sometimes children overhear adults say things when they are hurting that they don't mean, such as "I wish I had died;" or "I can't go on." It is enormously helpful in these moments to reassure them that adults, just like children, often speak rashly when they are sad and angry. While Janie and Nathan did not seem to fear the loss of their father through death, Janie was especially conflicted about not wanting her father to remarry, at the same time not wanting him to be lonely.

"Do you think Papa's lonely?" she asked me a few months after her mother's death.

"Yes, I think he is."

Janie began to cry. "I don't want him to be lonely, but I can't want him to get married either!"

"Janie, your father isn't interested in getting married now. I think that if a woman showed up on your doorstep looking for your father, he wouldn't know what to do!" She stopped crying and laughed.

"Your parents were married a long time. How would you expect one of them to feel if they lost the other? What your dad is feeling is normal, but he won't always feel this way. I suspect that when the time comes for him to meet someone else, you or Nathan will be the one fixing him up with the mother of someone you know."

"Cool," Janie said, and she reached for the TV remote control.

Children handle grief in many different ways. Some want to be alone while others want to be with lots of people; some let their grades drop and others have to make even better grades than they did before the loss; some hide their feelings and may become depressed and suicidal, and others "act out." While many can't remember details about the person who died, Janie was one of those who could access wonderful memories of her mother. She wrote in a college essay:

"My mom was the most caring and compassionate person I have ever met. It was very important for her to let my brother and me know every day how much we were loved. . . . My mom had this way of lifting me up into her lap and I would just fit. It was like her body was made to hold mine. My head always had a way of finding just the right spot on her enormous breasts and I would sit there with her holding me, feeling absolutely positive that she would protect me from the world. She was the softest person I know. She was soft in just the right places but strong enough to support me as I got older and just a little bit too big to fit in her lap. When I got too big to sit on her she would come over to me and just hug me. Not one of those pat-your-back hugs, but a gigantic bear hug that made me feel safe. She would just hold me like this and once again my head would find the perfect spot and her body would cradle mine. I have never felt as safe as I did in my mother's arms."

When acute sadness and grief turn into chronic depression or self-destructive acting out, special help may be needed. No matter how good the living parent is, he or she cannot be *both parents.* Sometimes the parent, as well as the children, may benefit from professional support. There is no shame in accepting this extra help. Janie and Nathan came to appreciate that, for them, it had been a wise thing to do.

"I have learned that you must rely on other people," Janie wrote. "Sometimes you have to ask for help and this only makes you stronger. People are here to help one another and it does not make you weaker to need assistance." Offering children this opportunity is part of the process of helping them find who they can confide in; who will help them feel better; who can comfort them the most.

As part of the grieving process leading to recovery, it is important that after a while children begin doing things that will make them feel good—the "going on" phase of the grief process. As children begin to live their own lives, they begin to envision a future that holds promise. Janie's reflections on that painful time during her freshman year in college illustrate this point:

"Less than one month shy of my fifteenth birthday, my mother passed away. This changed my whole world. I went through many difficult situations. My schoolwork suffered and so did my social life. I no longer wanted to hang out with my friends, but I wanted to be with my family even less. Everything I did or said reminded me of my mom, and people trying to comfort me seemed at times to make it worse. I even questioned my faith.

"When all of a sudden I was questioning everything I had ever been taught or believed, I was devastated. Having to overcome these fears and not knowing what or whom to believe was one of the most terrifying times of my life. When I finally realized that everything was going to be all right and not everything in the world had changed, I regained some of my faith in God and humankind. Because of these things I had felt, I decided to become an active participant in youth ministry. I now work with kids of all ages through my church and on the diocesan level. I get a lot out of this work and I have developed strong leadership skills."

Neither Janie nor Nathan could go into the church sanctuary for Sunday service for a long while after their mother's funeral. Janie ran the nursery each week, where she excelled in her commitment to children and received appreciation and affection from mothers who left their children in her care. After a few months, she would come into the sanctuary at the end of the service to receive communion. Occasionally, she would then go to the sacristy, where her mother's ashes were kept for several months in a small box encased in a green velvet pouch.

Nathan found his way through his grief in activities with the Boy Scouts. Eighteen months after his mother's death, he achieved the rank of Eagle Scout. His project involved building a memorial garden at his church. Later he won many service awards and was elected to national office in the Boy Scouts. He, too, reflected on lessons learned from his mother's death in an essay he wrote when he was a sophomore in college:

"I may only be twenty years old, but I feel like I have lived for quite a while. My best friend killed himself when we were freshmen in high school. Wow, talk about unwelcome emotions. All of a sudden, there I was, fourteen years old, and faced with the reality that some people are so unhappy that they want to die. Even worse, I learned that some people can get to that point, or at least think they are at that point, in only fourteen years. I didn't know what to do. Brian was the first 'one of us' to die in my life. Death became real, and life became confusing. I started worrying about other people dying, and I didn't know that this wasn't normal. I guess I figured that everyone worried about people dying. They don't.

"Brian killed himself in October, 1996. My mom died in January, 1997. Yeah, three months between two of the most painful, frustrating times of my life. I felt like people were just falling off, one by one. When my mom died, she took a piece of me with her. I don't think I will ever get that piece of myself back, but that's okay, because I kind of like feeling that she has part of me with her.

"I don't know that I have learned to live without my mom, but I have learned to live away from her. The rest of that year in high school was a joke. It's hard to take teachers seriously when you don't even know how to take life seriously. That was the end of my childhood. It's not as bad as it sounds though; it's allowed me to get good at being a grown-up. Life makes sense now, at least to me. I have begun to take control of my body and of myself. I am starting to believe that humans are the only animals that do not instinctively take care of themselves. What's even worse, in my opinion, is that people fail to take care of others as well. We should all, to a certain extent, be able to realize a calling to serve others.

"Life is not always as it seems; it's better. Today is my mother's birthday. I called my grandmother this morning, as I am sure that it must be rough, still, on her. She wasn't home, so I left a message on her answering machine. It's probably better that I did. This way, she can listen to it more than once if she wants to. It feels good to do things that help others, even if it's just something small. Can helping someone else ever really be something small?"

It takes most families about a year before they are ready to say a real good-bye to the person who has died. It had been fourteen months and Laura's ashes were still in the church's sacristy. The family was still divided over what to do with them. Laura's mother wanted the ashes buried next to Laura's father, who had died when she was twelve. Tim was sure Laura wanted her ashes scattered, not buried. We all knew that Laura wanted some of her ashes buried with Tim when he died.

The call came early one morning from Nathan. "Papa's taking the day off and we're driving up to the mountains to scatter Mom's ashes," he said.

"Is that all right with you?"

"If you three are ready, I think it's a great idea. What's the plan?"

"We've set some ashes aside to give to Grandma, and Janie and I have kept a few out to bury with Papa when he dies. The rest we're going to scatter at the top of a mountain. Don't you think that's what Mom would have wanted?"

"I really do. That would please your mom very much."

I was overwhelmed with an awareness that Janie and Nathan had learned the important lessons that their mother—and her death—had to teach them: they trusted people, they were curious, they were happy, and they were reaching out again to life with interest, enthusiasm and compassion.

Eda LeShan, in her memorable book *Learning to Say Good-by: When a Parent Dies,* tells the story of two young children who go back to visit their father's grave one year after his death. She describes reading a letter she'd written for the occasion to the girls' father—not really for him but for his daughters. When she finished reading this letter one of the young daughters looked very thoughtful, as if she was trying to think of some special message she would like to give to her father. Suddenly she ran and did a cartwheel on her daddy's grave. The widowed mother whispered to LeShan, "Liz hasn't done any cartwheels since Bob died. He used to love it when she did." LeShan realized that his daughter's gift to him "was to pick up the threads of her life and to begin to live as fully as she could. The time comes to begin to do cartwheels again—to express our joy in being alive."

I remembered LeShan's words as I noted the lightheartedness in Nathan's voice while he summarized the plans for their trip to the North Carolina mountains.

He called as soon as they returned.

"Leen, it was awesome!" he said.

"Tell me all about it."

"We got to the top of a mountain in the car and found a good place to pull off the road. It started to snow just as we stopped. We took the ashes and Janie read a little prayer. I said a few words, thanking Mom for all she did for us and telling her we loved her, and then Papa scooped up some ashes and scattered them in the snow. He really got his hands dirty! It was so beautiful! Then Janie and I started making snowballs and Janie mentioned how Mom had taught us how to make snow angels. She plopped down in the snow and began moving her arms and legs to make an angel. We started laughing and then we put some of Mom's ashes in snow balls and threw them down the mountain. It felt so good, and we knew she was laughing, too!"

57

Welcome Home

THERE'S MORE WE CAN LEARN from Janie and Nathan's story. "Leen, we have to move," Nathan said shortly after his mother's sudden death. "Sometimes the sadness hurts so bad I can feel it in my body. It's like a real pain. I don't want to be in this house," he said, tears running down his cheeks. "I don't even want to be in North Carolina. Let's ask Papa to put in for a transfer *anywhere*, and I'll go."

I held him close. "Nathan, let's look at the pros and cons, and if after we do that you still want to ask your dad if he would consider moving we can. But first I have to tell you that I can't move with you."

"You can't go? Why not?"

"Because my son lives here, my friends and my work are here, and this is where I've come to retire. And I can't think of any place I can go that will make me feel better about losing your mom. I have to get through this here with people who love me. I think you can, too."

"Well, that changes everything," Nathan said, hitting his forehead with the palm of his hand. "If you can't go, I have to rethink this whole thing!" Moving was never mentioned again. He worked through his grief, and healing took place in the home where death had turned his and Janie's world upside down.

Often it does not happen this way. When my friend's mother died, her father could not get out of the house fast enough. "He left that house as though it was on fire," she said. "He gave away family antiques, moved from place to place, and was never able to sleep or rest peacefully. He never dealt with his grief, never looked at inside issues, hoping instead that changing locations would improve his situation. It did not."

Once we feel at home in our own skins it is possible to take responsibility for creating an external home for ourselves. If we don't, it is difficult to feel secure anywhere, and we are likely to have problems wherever we go.

It is axiomatic that our "outer" and "inner" homes are very much related. There is a correlation between personality type and orientation to the physical home. For example, the intuitive personality type is not particularly observant of surroundings and not oriented to the physical world. The sensate person values things and enjoys collecting. The extrovert wants a home that accommodates lots of people and parties. The introvert does not think that way.

Many of us have sentimental attachments to our early living spaces. We organize our memories about our life experiences in relation to where we were living at the time. As a person whose parents moved ten or twelve times during my childhood, I identify early markers in my life by the house we were living in: I was born in the Lee House; I contracted diphtheria at the Wade Place. We had our first indoor plumbing and electricity at the McGee House, our first refrigerator at the Old Hill House. More than a half century later I still return occasionally to have a look at these dwellings.

Some of us are very attached to a place. Some would die for a piece of the good earth. Others believe that they can make their own home wherever they find themselves. It's not right or wrong; it's not an inferior or superior position to take. It's just one way to be in the world. The real question is what we know and understand about our inside home. If there is a mysterious disquiet with our home, perhaps we should look within. If we feel anxious with our house, it's likely to be an inside-ourselves problem.

I learned this lesson many years ago from a client whose story is instructive. "I always loved traveling," she said to me, "but each time I came home I had an anxiety attack. Even returning from work at the end of the day I felt a sick, anxious dread as I turned into the driveway. The apprehension that overcame me made no sense because I had a beautiful home, a garden that was the envy of the neighborhood, and a beautiful driveway entrance from the street."

Finally she understood that something was not right inside her. In therapy she discovered the 'inside' problem—a painful loss in her early childhood involving the death and burial of her beloved grandfather who had lived in their home and been her playmate. She had come home from kindergarten and found her grandfather gone. No one said anything to her, and when she finally asked her mother what had happened to her grandfather, her mother said through clenched teeth, "Don't upset your father." Neither parent mentioned the grandfather's name again.

Once she did her *internal* work, she no longer needed to improve her *external* surroundings, and the anxiety and dread disappeared. She discovered that if the home inside her skin was not light and joyful, no amount of money or square footage or landscaping or interior design could create a happy, peaceful place for her. Internal home improvement is sometimes costly and time-consuming. But the payoff is worth it. To feel truly at home is to be in harmony with oneself and one's environment. Sweeping the clutter from our internal abode gives us the freedom to connect to outside places and to feel at peace almost anywhere.

To paraphrase a familiar saying, when the going gets tough, the tough go home. When we are comfortable at our core, we can be at home within ourselves. It is said that "home is where the heart is." Perhaps it is more accurate to say that home is *in* the heart, and it is a heart-oriented job to become capable of making one's self at home. There we find the strength, courage, and wisdom to work through our problems, hanging in until healing comes.

58

Finding the Courage to Care

"GIVE ME THE MEDICINE THAT HELPS ME SLEEP," my friend's dying father said to her as she prepared to slip away for a few hours respite to join friends for dinner. A neighbor had arrived to sit with her father. She gave him the medication and saw fear on his drawn face.

"Please don't leave me," he whispered. She canceled her dinner plans and sent the neighbor home. She lay down on the bed beside her father and held his hand until he fell asleep. "It was an incredible moment," she would later tell me.

Being with a loved one through a terminal illness is one of life's most profound experiences. Taking this journey can be scary and unnerving. But to live life to the fullest, we must live it in its totality. That includes experiencing the death of those we cherish. Distance and circumstances may deprive us of being present during such times. But for those who do have the opportunity to participate fully in this awesome experience, facing death helps us grow into who we need to be.

While fear is normal, we can try to make sure that fear does not paralyze us. We can seek the courage and peace that will allow us to follow the person's needs and not impose our own agenda. When I asked another friend, Louise, what helped her most in caring for her dying brother, she replied, "First, I talked with a counselor to help me handle my deep personal grief. We sorted out accumulated issues from the past so I could approach the current situation with a clean slate." Often when we face the loss of a loved one, prior griefs revisit us, requiring us to take time to mourn earlier losses so that those do not intrude.

"Be light of foot," is what my Episcopal priest friend, Maxine, advises. She has kept vigil through the deaths of parishioners, her mother and her husband and she knows that each death is different from any other. For her, the value of touch is critical.

When Maxine's husband, Bill, died, she recalled, "well-intentioned nurses urged me not to stay with him once the ventilator was removed, telling me the experience would not be 'pleasant.' I knew that this wasn't about unpleasantness. I wasn't going to have him die alone. I climbed onto his hospital bed and held him through his last breath. Those last moments are some of my most vivid and painful images, but if I had it to do all over again, I would do the same thing. It changed me in profound ways. Telling the sufferer that you value and validate them is no less important in death than it is in life."

Themes of the importance of physical touch run deep in almost every story I know about being present when death is near. Elizabeth grew up with an alcoholic mother, and while she had worked on this in therapy, she did not experience profound healing until her mother was dying in a nursing home alone. After watching an aide begin to bathe her mother, Elizabeth sent the aide away. She tenderly bathed the frail, wrinkled, pain-wracked body. Her mother squeezed her hand. Elizabeth felt a peace she had not known. During the night her mother died.

My physician friend told me early into her father's illness that when it got to the point that he needed care with toileting, she would have to call someone else in. Too much intimacy made her uncomfortable. "I'm already having trouble that he's begun to leave the bathroom door open when he goes," she confided. Yet, when the time came, she allowed a tide of compassion to wash away that line in the sand and with great love and tenderness bathed and toileted her father until his death. She was able to be present in the moment, and that's what mattered.

Louise had the same experience with her brother. As his end neared, his care included holding the urinal and cleaning him when mishaps occurred. "We haven't been this close since we took baths together as kids," he whispered to her. They both smiled. Fear and embarrassment had been transformed into something profound and precious.

We need to experience life as long as there is life. If we begin the process of grieving too soon or try to rush it, we miss out. In order not to fall into this trap, we need to check in with ourselves from time to time. "How am I doing?" "How much help do I need?" "How is my support system?" We must not expect more of ourselves than we can give. If we take care of ourselves we can participate with our loved ones in this awesome and majestic process.

The sooner we are able to transform this experience into what it needs to be, the sooner we ourselves reap the benefits of having chosen to walk this path with someone we love. As we are present during the pending death of a loved one, we remind ourselves that, no matter what our belief systems, death is not the end. At the very least, the person will live on in our memories. We have the opportunity of making them comforting, healing ones by accepting and participating as fully in the process as we can.

Because the challenges are difficult for us adults, we may be tempted to shield our children. However, the age of the caretaker isn't always the critical issue. Of course, some children may need to be given permission *not* to participate if they feel too afraid. Not to worry. There will be other opportunities for these intense experiences that change us forever in wonderful ways.

59

Take My Hand

I TRIED TO IGNORE THE DULL ACHE in the pit of my stomach and to tell myself that the long flight was largely responsible for my sense of weariness. It was Christmas Eve and I was in a South Georgia nursing home near Roberta, where my eighty-eight-year-old mother was critically ill.

Precious Lord, take my hand...

The soloist at the traditional Christmas Eve service sang the popular spiritual in a voice reminiscent of Mahalia Jackson. Old people in wheelchairs moved closer to her. Attendants in starched white uniforms helped those who could still walk to comfortable seats.

Lead me on, let me stand . . .

I had a feeling of being engulfed, swallowed up, in the intense drama of the loneliness and the emptiness of once rich and vibrant lives. Nowhere was the reminder of the deep longing for human contact, warm hands, and friendly faces more strongly present than here, among the elderly, still reaching out to others, seeking to embrace life, even as their own slipped away.

I am tired, I am weak, I am worn . . .

After the service there arrived not one, but two Santas—a tall black man in a red suit and whiskers who joked with those able to move around the large social hall, and another Santa, the twelve-year-old daughter of one of the staff members, who handed out gifts to those assembled, bending carefully so as not to dislodge the basketball tied to her middle under her Santa suit. Nursing home staff members engaged in talk, which moved from the casual to the deeply personal.

Through the storm, through the night . . .

I walked the hallways to escape from the sounds of my semiconscious mother's discomfort as she slept and to stretch legs made weary from long, silent periods of bedside sitting. As I walked in a fog of sadness, I became aware of patients calling out to me.

"If you peel my orange, I'll give you a piece," a frail, stooped woman in a wheelchair whispered to me.

"If your mama's asleep, come in here and talk to me," begged another.

The residents within these walls represented a combined total of more than seven hundred years of living. With little prompting, they told their stories and their family secrets. Tears and laughter flowed unashamedly; hands reached out to clutch mine.

"You sure do know how to make your mother feel good," Mama's slight, ninety-nine-year-old roommate, Cora, whispered in my ear as I bathed my mother's face. "Can you make me feel better, too?" Her smile revealed teeth rotted with age and tobacco stains. I touched her wrinkled hand and smiled back at her. Later, I joined Cora in the parade of wheelchairs heading to a small reception area where a four-foot plastic tree twinkled in a corner.

Christmas gifts were opened and everyone expressed appreciation for each bottle of lotion, box of candy, container of bath powder, flannel nightgown, and jar of hard candies.

Lead me on to the light . . .

I realized just how limited are the choices for gifts for people in a nursing home. I was also aware that some patients had received nothing from their families, but caring staff members had lovingly bought and wrapped gifts for them and placed them under the tree in the front lobby.

The early evening hours were quiet. The corridors were empty. Sleep, however restless, came quickly to those tired by all the day's activities. As the morning sun began to peek through the blinds and people began to stir and to greet each other with "Merry Christmas," word spread quietly through the building that there was one fewer patient there to greet Christmas Day.

Visitors and gifts continued to arrive. Young girls dressed in Brownie uniforms walked the halls singing, "We are the happy Brownies / we are the happy Elves / We like to help each other / and of course we help ourselves." They stopped at each door, entered quietly, and left each resident a stick of gum and a piece of candy wrapped in bright red cellophane.

Small bags of fruit arrived from the Friendship Circle of the True Faith Baptist Church. Molasses cookies were delivered by members of the Golden Age Club of the United Methodist Church. The nursing home chaplain and his wife brought assorted homemade candies and cookies on paper plates.

There was joy and pride on the faces of those who received visits from family members and old friends, delight on the faces of those few who could be taken home for the day. Those without visitors either made attempts to explain why no one was able to visit them, or simply acknowledged that they had outlived other members of their family. But curiosity and anticipation ran high each time that new footsteps were heard in the hall.

It was late afternoon on Christmas Day. Watching the staff make their rounds—checking temperatures, giving medications, stopping to talk with visitors—I realized that there was something unique and warm and tender in this place. I leaned my head back and closed my eyes, trying to absorb it all.

In this tiny space in a small Georgia town, a town in which I had grown up but left more than two decades before, blacks and whites were working together, living together, laughing together, in a way I had not witnessed growing up in this little community.

White patients whose grandparents had been slaveholders and who had needed reassurance upon their arrival that they would not have to share toilets with "colored people" were now sharing the most intimate details of their lives with black patients and staff. Age, illness, loneliness, the longing for human contact had been the great leveler.

There was no room, no time for hatred or distrust or pettiness. The staff sensed this, and so did the patients and guests. The affection was genuinely sought and freely given, and I became aware that I was caught up in it, both as a giver and a receiver. And I was grateful for the balm it provided my sagging spirits.

I closed my eyes and allowed memories to flood my mind. Mama was married at age eighteen, and her first child was born two years later. Twenty years later she gave birth to her ninth and final child. None of us had ever heard Mama talk about childbirth or about labor pains. All her children had been delivered at home, without benefit of pain relief. Mama was silent on the trials of childbirth, even when other women on the farm had babies and shared their stories of pain.

It was not until our last Christmas day together that I heard Mama make the connection between birth and pain. Semiconscious, wracked with a fever and severe stomach distress, she reached for my hand and pulled me close. "Is the baby about ready to come out?" she whispered in my ear. "It's been a long time."

I squeezed her hand. "Yes, mama, it will soon be over," I assured her as the nurse gave her pain medication.

“I want you to promise me you’ll take care of the baby,” she said, before drifting back into unconsciousness.

“I promise,” I whispered. “You don’t have to worry.” She gave a slight nod of her head. Sharing such an intimacy with my mother gave me an inexplicable feeling of love and joy and peace. I was able to let go.

“I’m sorry, but there’s no way your mother’s going to be any better,” the doctor told me as we stood outside my mother’s door. I had known him since I was a teenager. “I’ll take good care of her and make her comfortable, so don’t worry about that when you have to go back up to Boston.” He gave me a hug and walked away, late for Christmas dinner with his own family.

Visitors began to leave, and the air was filled with the final calls of “Merry Christmas.” Many of the patients were already napping. Down the hall I heard the rattling of trays being removed from the dinner cart. I stretched my legs, got a cup of coffee from the kitchen, and returned to my mother’s bedside, reassured that her sleep was then peaceful.

Take my hand, precious Lord, lead me home.

Epilogue

Acting on the Knack

"LIFE IS EITHER A DARING ADVENTURE OR NOTHING," Helen Keller said. She should know. Deaf, blind, and mute after suffering "brain fever" as an infant in 1882, she pushed the limits of her silent world to the max by learning to communicate, graduating from Radcliffe College and traveling the world promoting education for the handicapped and social justice. It was part of her humanness to strive, to seek challenge, to take risks in the hope of favorable outcomes.

Human history is the story of adventures. Think of the early explorers, those bold souls in boats setting out to find what lay across the ocean. Today, adventure is for sale in the form of a Ford Explorer and jillions of other products and services pandering to that innate drive. We live today in a time when, for most of us, our basic needs for food, clothing, and shelter are met. We are free to seek stimulation through lifelong learning, exotic food, extreme sports and travel, not to mention the endless virtual excitement available on the World Wide Web.

Psychologist Abraham Maslow suggests that when all other needs are at least superficially met, we seek adventure and variety as a part of becoming self-actualized. Self-actualization is what brings joy. The ideal is to enjoy variety, to benefit from new challenges, without being obsessively driven and without taking self-defeating risks.

Different people have different needs for sensation. For physical and psychological reasons, some nervous systems need soothing harmony and others need much stimulation. Sometimes this difference in needs can present challenges to relationships. My friend Leslie has always been an adventurer, traveling around the world, studying languages, teaching in foreign countries. These explorations were fed in part by her fiery temperament and a need to escape a painful childhood. Her gentle, sensitive husband, who does not have strong sensation needs, grew up in a stable, loving environment. Now when a new restaurant opens, Leslie wants to be the first to try it out. Her husband likes to go repeatedly to the local café. He knows what he will order there and how much it will cost. Leslie insists on trying the new place, and her loving husband grits his teeth and goes along with her plan.

"I'll just think of this as an adventure. When the check comes, I'll pretend we're in Paris." Then, with a smile he adds, "But I sure hope we don't have to do this again soon. Next time let's go somewhere old!"

Life is difficult enough without taking chances when the statistics are against us. We wear ourselves out, expend enormous amounts of energy, and sacrifice important relationships if we stay in a whirlwind of stimulation. People who have a high need for excitement and drama can stir up negative energy and create problems without realizing it. What each person needs is "just right" simulation for him or her. Unsatisfying, repetitive thrill seeking arises from uncontrolled, unconscious drives. On the other hand, bold, courageous acts flow naturally from certain personalities who go through a process of balancing needs, interests, desires, skills, and solid preparation.

Risk-taking is not the same as being irresponsible. There is a continuum of balance between being driven by neurotic, unproductive, unconscious needs run amok, and the creative risk-taking balanced by skills mastery. The Indian spiritual master Meher Baba tells us that humanity suffers from insatiable desire: "People who can find no peace or rest seek to forget themselves in excitement." The irony is that in seeking to avoid suffering through an unhealthy approach to adventure-seeking, we bring more suffering on ourselves and on others.

There is no end to the possibilities for external stimulation. There is always one more place to visit, one more food to taste, one more relationship to try. In order to derive peace of mind and lasting joy, what we need is the awareness that inwardly we can find what is important. Again quoting from Meher Baba, "When mind soars in pursuit of the things in space, it pursues emptiness, but when man dives deep within himself he experiences the fullness of existence."

I like to look at "adventure" a little like a venture capitalist might—as an investment of energy from which I have reasonable expectation of benefit. I don't want to throw my energy away by not considering the outcome before I invest. Neither do I want to conserve energy to the point of boredom and uselessness. Because I am a human being, like Helen Keller, I am an adventurer. It's no big deal—just a part of life. To the extent I can be aware, I can choose the *ventures* I *add* to my life. If I am aware, I will be less likely to take unhealthy chances emanating from unconscious drives.

The "just-right" adventure includes delving inside ourselves and finding that it is not so much that we are in an exciting world—but that an exciting world of resources exists within us.

This book was composed in
Adobe InDesign CS2 for the Macintosh computer.
The text was composed in the Minion family of fonts,
designed by Robert Slimbach; Zapfino, by Hermann Zapf;
and Birch, by Kim Buker Chansler, three modern
masters of typography.

Printed in the United States
200802BV00002B/307/A

9 780978 973636